ONE POT
ONE PAN
ONE DISH

pil

Publications International, Ltd.

Pictured on the front cover: Sheet Pan Chicken and Sausage Supper (*page 108*) and Hearty Hash Brown Casserole (*page 18*).

Pictured on the back cover (*clockwise from top left*): Sausage, Potato and Apple Bake (*page 104*), Corned Beef and Cabbage Soup (*page 26*), and Smoked Salmon Omelet (*page 5*).

ISBN: 978-1-64558-744-6

Manufactured in China.

8 7 6 5 4 3 2 1

Microwave Cooking: Microwave ovens vary in wattage. Use the cooking times as guidelines and check for doneness before adding more time.

WARNING: Food preparation, baking and cooking involve inherent dangers: misuse of electric products, sharp electric tools, boiling water, hot stoves, allergic reactions, foodborne illnesses and the like, pose numerous potential risks. Publications International, Ltd. (PIL) assumes no responsibility or liability for any damages you may experience as a result of following recipes, instructions, tips or advice in this publication.

While we hope this publication helps you find new ways to eat delicious foods, you may not always achieve the results desired due to variations in ingredients, cooking temperatures, typos, errors, omissions or individual cooking abilities.

Let's get social!
@Publications_International
@PublicationsInternational
www.pilbooks.com

TABLE OF CONTENTS

BEST BREAKFASTS

SMOKED SALMON OMELET

MAKES 1 SERVING

- 3 eggs
- 2 tablespoons milk
- 1 tablespoon grated Parmesan cheese
  Pinch white or black pepper
- 1 teaspoon butter
- 2 tablespoons finely chopped red onion, divided
- 1 ounce smoked salmon, cut into 1- to 2-inch pieces
- 2 tablespoons sour cream
- 1 tablespoon water
- 1 tablespoon capers, rinsed and drained
  Finely chopped fresh parsley (optional)

---

1. Whisk eggs, milk, Parmesan cheese and pepper in small bowl until well blended.

2. Heat butter in small (6-inch) nonstick skillet over medium-high heat. Pour egg mixture into skillet; stir briefly. Let eggs begin to set at edges, then lift edges and tilt skillet, allowing uncooked portion of egg mixture to flow underneath. Cook about 1 minute or until omelet begins to set. Sprinkle 1 tablespoon onion over half of omelet; top with smoked salmon. Fold other half of omelet over filling; cook about 1 minute. Slide omelet onto serving plate.

3. Whisk sour cream and water in small bowl until blended. Drizzle over omelet; top with remaining 1 tablespoon onion, capers and parsley, if desired.

QUINOA BREAKFAST "FRIED RICE"

MAKES 4 SERVINGS

2 tablespoons vegetable oil, divided

1 carrot, finely diced

¾ cup frozen peas

4 ounces deli ham, finely diced (optional)

2 green onions, thinly sliced

2 teaspoons minced garlic

1 teaspoon grated ginger

3 eggs, lightly beaten

⅛ teaspoon kosher salt

4 cups cooked quinoa

1 tablespoon reduced-sodium soy sauce, plus additional for serving

1 tablespoon ketchup

¼ teaspoon freshly ground black pepper

1. Heat 1 tablespoon oil in large nonstick skillet over medium-high heat. Add carrot and peas; cook about 4 minutes or until softened. Add ham, if desired; cook about 2 minutes or until lightly browned. Add green onions, garlic and ginger; cook about 1 minute or until fragrant. Transfer to large bowl.

2. Heat remaining 1 tablespoon oil in skillet over medium-high heat. Add eggs and salt; cook about 1 minute or until lightly scrambled and set. Break up eggs into small, bite-size pieces with spatula.

3. Return carrot-pea mixture to skillet. Add quinoa; cook and stir 2 minutes. Add 1 tablespoon soy sauce, ketchup and pepper; cook and stir 1 minute or until heated through. Serve with additional soy sauce, if desired.

NOTE: To prepare quinoa, place 1 cup uncooked quinoa, 1½ cups water and ¼ teaspoon salt in large saucepan; bring to a boil over medium-high heat. Reduce heat to low; cover and cook about 15 minutes or until quinoa is tender and water is absorbed. Cool completely. Or, if preferred, you can prepare the quinoa in advance and refrigerate.

BREAKFAST BISCUIT BAKE

MAKES 8 SERVINGS

8 ounces bacon, chopped

1 small onion, finely chopped

1 clove garlic, minced

¼ teaspoon red pepper flakes

5 eggs

¼ cup milk

½ cup (2 ounces) shredded white Cheddar cheese, divided

¼ teaspoon salt

⅛ teaspoon black pepper

1 package (16 ounces) refrigerated jumbo buttermilk biscuits (8 biscuits)

1. Preheat oven to 425°F. Cook bacon in large cast iron skillet until crisp. Remove to paper towel-lined plate. Drain and reserve drippings, leaving 1 tablespoon in skillet.

2. Add onion, garlic and red pepper flakes to skillet; cook and stir 8 minutes or until onion is softened. Set aside to cool slightly.

3. Whisk eggs, milk, ¼ cup cheese, salt and black pepper in medium bowl until well blended. Stir in onion mixture.

4. Wipe out any onion mixture remaining in skillet; grease with additional drippings, if necessary. Separate biscuits and arrange in single layer in bottom of skillet. (Bottom of skillet should be completely covered.) Pour egg mixture over biscuits; sprinkle with remaining ¼ cup cheese and cooked bacon.

5. Bake about 25 minutes or until puffed and golden brown. Serve warm.

ROASTED PEPPER AND SOURDOUGH BRUNCH CASSEROLE

MAKES 8 SERVINGS

---

3 cups sourdough bread cubes

1 jar (12 ounces) roasted red pepper strips, drained

1 cup (4 ounces) shredded reduced-fat sharp Cheddar cheese

1 cup (4 ounces) shredded reduced-fat Monterey Jack cheese

1 cup fat-free cottage cheese

1½ cups cholesterol-free egg substitute

1 cup fat-free (skim) milk

¼ cup chopped fresh cilantro

¼ teaspoon black pepper

---

1. Lightly coat 11×7-inch baking dish with nonstick cooking spray. Place bread cubes in prepared baking dish; top with roasted peppers, Cheddar and Monterey Jack cheese.

2. Place cottage cheese in food processor or blender; process until smooth. Add egg substitute and milk; process just until blended. Pour over ingredients in baking dish. Sprinkle with cilantro and black pepper. Cover and refrigerate 4 hours or overnight.

3. Preheat oven to 375°F. Bake, uncovered, 40 minutes or until center is set and top is golden brown.

FABULOUS FETA FRITTATA

8 **eggs**

¼ **cup plain nonfat Greek yogurt**

¼ **cup chopped fresh basil**

¼ **teaspoon salt**

¼ **teaspoon black pepper**

1 **tablespoon olive oil or butter**

1 **package (4 ounces) crumbled feta cheese with basil, olives and sun-dried tomatoes** *or* **1 cup crumbled plain feta cheese**

¼ **cup pine nuts (optional)**

1. Preheat broiler. Beat eggs, yogurt, basil, salt and pepper in medium bowl.

2. Heat oil in large ovenproof skillet over medium heat, tilting skillet to coat bottom and side. Pour egg mixture into skillet; cover and cook 8 to 10 minutes or until eggs are set around edge (center will be wet).

3. Sprinkle feta and pine nuts, if desired, evenly over top. Transfer to broiler; broil 4 to 5 inches from heat source 2 minutes or until center is set and pine nuts are golden brown. Cut into wedges.

TIP: This frittata also makes a great meal. Cut it into quarters and serve it hot with fruit for breakfast, tuck a wedge into half a pita for lunch, or serve it alongside roasted red potatoes for dinner.

GERMAN APPLE PANCAKE

MAKES 6 SERVINGS

1 tablespoon butter

1 large or 2 small apples, peeled and thinly sliced (about 1½ cups)

1 tablespoon packed brown sugar

1½ teaspoons ground cinnamon, divided

2 eggs

2 egg whites

1 tablespoon granulated sugar

1 teaspoon vanilla

¼ teaspoon salt

½ cup all-purpose flour

½ cup milk

Maple syrup (optional)

1. Preheat oven to 425°F.

2. Melt butter in medium cast iron or ovenproof skillet* over medium heat. Add apples, brown sugar and ½ teaspoon cinnamon; cook and stir 5 minutes or until apples just begin to soften. Remove from heat. Arrange apple slices in single layer in skillet.

3. Whisk eggs, egg whites, granulated sugar, remaining 1 teaspoon cinnamon, vanilla and salt in medium bowl until well blended. Stir in flour and milk until smooth and well blended. Pour evenly over apples.

4. Bake 20 to 25 minutes or until puffed and golden brown. Serve with maple syrup, if desired.

*To make skillet ovenproof, wrap handle in foil.

NOTE: Pancake will fall slightly after being removed from the oven.

EDAMAME FRITTATA

MAKES 4 SERVINGS

---

2 tablespoons olive oil

½ cup frozen shelled edamame

⅓ cup frozen corn

¼ cup chopped shallot (1 shallot)

5 eggs

¾ teaspoon Italian seasoning

½ teaspoon salt

½ teaspoon black pepper

¼ cup chopped green onions

½ cup crumbled goat cheese

---

1. Preheat broiler. Heat oil in large ovenproof nonstick skillet over medium-high heat. Add edamame, corn and shallot; cook and stir 6 to 8 minutes or until shallot is lightly browned and edamame are hot.

2. Meanwhile, beat eggs, Italian seasoning, salt and pepper in medium bowl. Stir in green onions. Pour egg mixture over vegetables in skillet. Sprinkle with cheese. Cook over medium heat 5 to 7 minutes or until eggs are set on bottom, gently lifting up mixture to allow uncooked portion to flow underneath.

3. Broil 6 inches from heat 1 minute or until top is puffy and golden brown. Loosen frittata from skillet with spatula; slide onto small platter. Cut into wedges.

HEARTY HASH BROWN CASSEROLE

MAKES ABOUT 16 SERVINGS

- 2 cups sour cream
- 2 cups (8 ounces) shredded Colby cheese, divided
- 1 can (10¾ ounces) cream of chicken soup
- ½ cup (1 stick) butter, melted
- 1 small onion, finely chopped
- ¾ teaspoon salt
- ½ teaspoon black pepper
- 1 package (30 ounces) frozen shredded hash brown potatoes, thawed

1. Preheat oven to 375°F. Spray 13×9-inch baking dish with nonstick cooking spray.

2. Combine sour cream, 1½ cups cheese, soup, butter, onion, salt and pepper in large bowl; mix well. Add potatoes; stir until well blended. Spread mixture in prepared baking dish. (Do not pack down.) Sprinkle with remaining ½ cup cheese.

3. Bake 45 minutes or until cheese is melted and top of casserole is beginning to brown.

SOOTHING SOUPS & MORE

TURKEY CHILI

MAKES ABOUT 8 SERVINGS

2 tablespoons olive oil, divided

2 pounds ground turkey

2 onions, chopped

2 stalks celery, chopped

2 medium carrots, chopped

2 cloves garlic, minced

2 tablespoons chili powder

2 teaspoons ground cumin

1½ teaspoons salt

1 teaspoon Italian seasoning

1 teaspoon red pepper flakes

½ teaspoon black pepper

2 tablespoons tomato paste

1 can (28 ounces) tomato purée

1 container (32 ounces) chicken or vegetable broth

1 can (about 15 ounces) chickpeas

1 can (about 15 ounces) kidney beans

¾ cup corn (thawed if frozen)

¾ cup edamame (thawed if frozen)

1. Heat 1 tablespoon oil in large saucepan or Dutch oven over medium-high heat. Add turkey; cook about 8 minutes or until no longer pink, stirring to break up meat. Remove to medium bowl; drain off any excess liquid.

2. Add remaining 1 tablespoon oil, onions, celery and carrots to saucepan; cook about 10 minutes or until vegetables are softened, stirring frequently. Add garlic; cook and stir 1 minute. Add chili powder, cumin, salt, Italian seasoning, red pepper flakes and black pepper; cook and stir 1 minute. Add tomato paste; cook and stir 1 minute.

3. Return turkey to saucepan with tomato purée; mix well. Stir in broth and bring to a boil. Reduce heat to low; cook, uncovered, 30 minutes.

4. Add chickpeas, beans, corn and edamame; cook 20 minutes, stirring occasionally.

SUMMER CORN CHOWDER

MAKES 6 SERVINGS

5 ears corn, shucked

2 tablespoons butter

1 medium onion, chopped

1 large poblano pepper, diced (¼-inch pieces)

2 cloves garlic, minced

1 container (32 ounces) chicken or vegetable broth

1½ teaspoons salt, divided

½ teaspoon black pepper, divided

¼ teaspoon ground red pepper

1 pound red potatoes, peeled and cut into ½-inch pieces

3 plum tomatoes, diced (about 2 cups)

½ cup whipping cream

2 tablespoons lime juice

2 tablespoons chopped fresh cilantro

¼ cup crumbled crisp-cooked bacon (optional)

1. Cut kernels off cobs; place in medium bowl. Working over bowl, run back of knife up and down cobs to release additional corn pulp and milk from cobs into bowl. Break cobs in half; set aside.

2. Melt butter in large saucepan or Dutch oven over medium heat. Add onion, poblano pepper and garlic; cook about 5 minutes or until vegetables are softened, stirring occasionally. Stir in broth, 1 teaspoon salt, ¼ teaspoon black pepper and red pepper; mix well. Add corn cobs; bring to a boil. Reduce heat to medium-low; cover and cook 15 minutes.

3. Stir in potatoes; cover and cook 20 minutes. Stir in corn and tomatoes; cook, uncovered, 20 minutes. Remove and discard corn cobs. Coarsely mash soup with potato masher. (Or use immersion blender to briefly blend soup just until slightly chunky.)

4. Stir in cream; cook 3 minutes or until heated through. Stir in lime juice, cilantro, remaining ½ teaspoon salt and ¼ teaspoon pepper. Garnish with bacon.

SALSA VERDE CHICKEN STEW

MAKES 4 TO 6 SERVINGS

---

1 tablespoon vegetable oil

1½ pounds boneless skinless chicken breasts, cut into ¾-inch pieces

2 cans (about 15 ounces each) black beans, rinsed and drained

1 jar (24 ounces) salsa verde

1½ cups frozen corn

¾ cup chopped fresh cilantro

Diced avocado (optional)

---

1. Heat oil in large saucepan over medium-high heat. Add chicken; cook and stir about 5 minutes or until chicken begins to brown.

2. Stir in beans and salsa; bring to a simmer. Reduce heat to low; cover and cook 8 minutes.

3. Stir in corn; cook, uncovered, about 3 minutes or until heated through. Remove from heat; stir in cilantro. Garnish with avocado; serve with tortilla chips, if desired.

CORNED BEEF AND CABBAGE SOUP

MAKES ABOUT 8 SERVINGS

---

1 tablespoon vegetable oil

1 onion, chopped

2 stalks celery, chopped

2 carrots, chopped

2 cloves garlic, minced

4 to 5 cups coarsely chopped green cabbage (about half of small head)

12 ounces unpeeled Yukon gold potatoes, chopped

4 cups beef broth

4 cups water

½ cup quick-cooking barley

1 teaspoon salt

1 teaspoon dried thyme

½ teaspoon black pepper

¼ teaspoon ground mustard

12 ounces corned beef (leftovers or deli corned beef, about 2½ cups), cut into ½-inch pieces

---

1. Heat oil in large saucepan or Dutch oven over medium-high heat. Add onion, celery and carrots; cook 5 minutes or until vegetables are softened, stirring occasionally. Add garlic; cook and stir 1 minute.

2. Stir in cabbage, potatoes, broth, water, barley, 1 teaspoon salt, thyme, ½ teaspoon pepper and mustard; bring to a boil. Reduce heat to medium-low. Cook 20 minutes, stirring occasionally.

3. Stir in corned beef; cook 10 to 15 minutes or until potatoes are tender. Season with additional salt and pepper, if desired.

LENTIL SOUP

MAKES 6 TO 8 SERVINGS

---

2 tablespoons olive oil, divided

2 medium onions, chopped

1½ teaspoons salt

4 cloves garlic, minced

¼ cup tomato paste

1 teaspoon dried oregano

½ teaspoon dried basil

¼ teaspoon dried thyme

¼ teaspoon black pepper

½ cup dry sherry or white wine

8 cups vegetable broth

2 cups water

3 carrots, cut into ½-inch pieces

2 cups dried lentils, rinsed and sorted

1 cup chopped fresh parsley

1 tablespoon balsamic vinegar

---

1. Heat 1 tablespoon oil in large saucepan or Dutch oven over medium heat. Add onions; cook 10 minutes, stirring occasionally. Add remaining 1 tablespoon oil and salt; cook 10 minutes or until onions are golden brown, stirring frequently.

2. Add garlic; cook and stir 1 minute. Add tomato paste, oregano, basil, thyme and pepper; cook and stir 1 minute. Stir in sherry; cook 30 seconds, scraping up browned bits from bottom of saucepan.

3. Stir in broth, water, carrots and lentils; cover and bring to a boil over high heat. Reduce heat to medium-low; cook, partially covered, 30 minutes or until lentils are tender.

4. Remove from heat; stir in parsley and vinegar.

PEPPERY SICILIAN CHICKEN SOUP

MAKES 8 TO 10 SERVINGS

2 tablespoons olive oil

1 onion, chopped

1 green bell pepper, chopped

3 stalks celery, chopped

3 carrots, chopped

3 cloves garlic, minced

1 tablespoon salt

3 containers (32 ounces each) chicken broth

2 pounds boneless skinless chicken breasts

1 can (28 ounces) diced tomatoes

2 baking potatoes, peeled and cut into ¼-inch pieces

1½ teaspoons ground white pepper*

1½ teaspoons ground black pepper

½ cup chopped fresh parsley

2 cups cooked ditalini pasta

Or substitute additional black pepper for the white pepper.

1. Heat oil in large saucepan or Dutch oven over medium heat. Stir in onion, bell pepper, celery and carrots. Reduce heat to medium-low; cover and cook 10 to 15 minutes or until vegetables are tender but not browned, stirring occasionally. Stir in garlic and 1 tablespoon salt; cover and cook 5 minutes.

2. Stir in broth, chicken, tomatoes, potatoes, white pepper and black pepper; bring to a boil. Reduce heat to low; cover and simmer 1 hour. Remove chicken to plate; set aside until cool enough to handle. Shred chicken and return to saucepan with parsley.

3. Add pasta to soup. Taste and season with additional salt, if desired.

NOTE: Prepare pasta in advance according to package directions. Eight ounces uncooked pasta makes about 2 cups cooked.

ITALIAN WEDDING SOUP

MAKES 8 SERVINGS

MEATBALLS

- 2 eggs
- 2 cloves garlic, minced
- 1 teaspoon salt
- ⅛ teaspoon black pepper
- 1½ pounds meat loaf mix (ground beef and pork)
- ¾ cup plain dry bread crumbs
- ½ cup grated Parmesan cheese
- 2 tablespoons olive oil

SOUP

- 1 onion, chopped
- 2 carrots, chopped
- 4 cloves garlic, minced
- 2 heads escarole or curly endive, coarsely chopped
- 8 cups chicken broth
- 1 can (about 14 ounces) Italian plum tomatoes, undrained, coarsely chopped
- 3 sprigs fresh thyme
- 1 teaspoon salt
- ½ teaspoon red pepper flakes
- 1 cup uncooked acini di pepe pasta

1. Whisk eggs, 2 cloves garlic, 1 teaspoon salt and black pepper in large bowl until blended. Stir in meat loaf mix, bread crumbs and Parmesan cheese; mix gently until well blended. Shape mixture by tablespoonfuls into 1-inch balls.

2. Heat oil in large saucepan or Dutch oven over medium heat. Cook meatballs in batches 5 minutes or until browned. Remove to plate; set aside.

3. Add onion, carrots and 4 cloves garlic to saucepan; cook and stir 5 minutes or until onion is lightly browned. Add escarole; cook 2 minutes or until wilted. Stir in broth, tomatoes with juice, thyme, 1 teaspoon salt and red pepper flakes; bring to a boil over high heat. Reduce heat to medium-low; cook 15 minutes.

4. Add meatballs and pasta to soup; return to a boil over high heat. Reduce heat to medium; cook 10 minutes or until pasta is tender. Remove and discard thyme sprigs before serving.

BROCCOLI CHEESE SOUP

MAKES 4 TO 6 SERVINGS

- 6 tablespoons (¾ stick) butter
- 1 cup chopped onion
- 1 clove garlic, minced
- ¼ cup all-purpose flour
- 2 cups vegetable broth
- 2 cups milk
- 1½ teaspoons Dijon mustard
- ½ teaspoon salt
- ¼ teaspoon ground nutmeg
- ¼ teaspoon black pepper
- ⅛ teaspoon hot pepper sauce
- 1 package (16 ounces) frozen broccoli (5 cups)
- 2 carrots, shredded (1 cup)
- 6 ounces pasteurized process cheese product, cubed
- 1 cup (4 ounces) shredded sharp Cheddar cheese, plus additional for garnish

---

1. Melt butter in large saucepan or Dutch oven over medium-low heat. Add onion; cook and stir 8 minutes or until softened. Add garlic; cook and stir 1 minute. Increase heat to medium. Whisk in flour until smooth; cook and stir 3 minutes without browning.

2. Gradually whisk in broth and milk. Add mustard, salt, nutmeg, black pepper and hot pepper sauce; cook 15 minutes or until thickened, stirring occasionally.

3. Add broccoli; cook 15 minutes. Add carrots; cook 10 minutes or until vegetables are tender.

4. Transfer half of soup to food processor or blender; process until smooth. Return to saucepan. Add cheese product and 1 cup Cheddar; cook and stir over low heat until cheese is melted. Ladle into bowls; garnish with additional Cheddar.

ONE-POT CHINESE CHICKEN SOUP

MAKES 4 SERVINGS

---

6 cups chicken broth

2 cups water

1 pound boneless skinless chicken thighs

⅓ cup reduced-sodium soy sauce

1 package (16 ounces) frozen stir-fry vegetables

6 ounces uncooked dried thin Chinese egg noodles

1 to 3 tablespoons sriracha sauce

---

1. Combine broth, water, chicken and soy sauce in medium saucepan; bring to a boil over high heat. Reduce heat to low; cover and simmer about 20 minutes or until chicken is cooked through and very tender. Remove to bowl; let stand until cool enough to handle.

2. Meanwhile, add vegetables and noodles to broth in saucepan; bring to a boil over high heat. Reduce heat to medium-high; cook about 5 minutes or until noodles are tender and vegetables are heated through, stirring frequently.

3. Shred chicken into bite-size pieces. Stir chicken and 1 tablespoon sriracha into soup; taste and add additional sriracha for a spicier flavor.

GARDEN VEGETABLE SOUP

MAKES 8 TO 10 SERVINGS

1 tablespoon olive oil

1 medium onion, chopped

1 carrot, chopped

1 stalk celery, chopped

1 medium zucchini, diced

1 medium yellow squash, diced

1 red bell pepper, diced

2 tablespoons tomato paste

2 cloves garlic, minced

2 teaspoons salt

1 teaspoon Italian seasoning

½ teaspoon black pepper

8 cups vegetable broth

1 can (28 ounces) whole tomatoes, chopped, juice reserved

½ cup uncooked pearl barley

1 cup cut green beans (1-inch pieces)

½ cup corn

¼ cup slivered fresh basil

1 tablespoon lemon juice

1. Heat oil in large saucepan or Dutch oven over medium-high heat. Add onion, carrot and celery; cook and stir 8 minutes or until vegetables are softened. Add zucchini, yellow squash and bell pepper; cook and stir 5 minutes or until softened. Stir in tomato paste, garlic, salt, Italian seasoning and black pepper; cook 1 minute. Stir in broth and tomatoes with juice; bring to a boil. Stir in barley.

2. Reduce heat to low; cook 30 minutes. Stir in green beans and corn; cook about 15 minutes or until barley is tender and green beans are crisp-tender. Stir in basil and lemon juice.

WHITE BEAN AND CHICKEN RAGOÛT

MAKES 2 SERVINGS

---

2 boneless skinless chicken thighs

2 small carrots, cut into ½-inch pieces

2 medium celery stalks, cut into ½-inch pieces

¼ medium onion, chopped

1 bay leaf

1 sprig fresh parsley

1 clove garlic

1 sprig fresh thyme

3 black peppercorns

1 cup cooked cannellini beans

1 plum tomato, chopped

1 teaspoon herbes de Provence

½ teaspoon salt

⅛ teaspoon black pepper

1 teaspoon extra virgin olive oil

1 tablespoon chopped fresh parsley

Grated peel of 1 lemon

---

1. Place chicken in medium saucepan; add water to cover. Add carrots, celery, onion, bay leaf, parsley, garlic, thyme and peppercorns. Bring to a boil over high heat; reduce heat to low. Simmer 15 to 20 minutes or until vegetables are tender.

2. Remove chicken to plate; let cool 5 minutes.

3. Drain vegetables; reserve broth. Remove and discard bay leaf, parsley, garlic, thyme and peppercorns.

4. Cut chicken into bite-size pieces when cool enough to handle. Return chicken and vegetables to saucepan. Stir in beans, tomato, herbes de Provence, salt, black pepper and 1 cup reserved broth. Simmer 5 minutes.

5. Divide ragoût between two bowls; drizzle with oil. Sprinkle with chopped parsley and lemon peel.

ALL-IN-ONE BURGER STEW

MAKES 6 SERVINGS

---

1 pound lean ground beef

2 cups frozen Italian-style vegetables

1 can (about 14 ounces) diced tomatoes with basil and garlic

1 can (about 14 ounces) beef broth

2½ cups uncooked medium egg noodles

Salt and black pepper

---

1. Brown beef in Dutch oven or large skillet over medium-high heat 6 to 8 minutes, stirring to break up meat. Drain fat.

2. Add vegetables, tomatoes and broth; bring to a boil over high heat.

3. Stir in noodles. Reduce heat to medium; cover and cook 12 to 15 minutes or until vegetables and noodles are tender. Season with salt and pepper.

NOTE: For a special touch, sprinkle with chopped parsley before serving.

TIP: To complete this meal, serve with breadsticks or a loaf of Italian bread and a simple salad.

VEGGIE BEEF SKILLET SOUP

MAKES 4 SERVINGS

¾ **pound ground beef**

1 **tablespoon olive oil**

2 **cups coarsely chopped cabbage**

1 **cup chopped green bell pepper**

2 **cups water**

1 **can (about 14 ounces) stewed tomatoes**

1 **cup frozen mixed vegetables**

⅓ **cup ketchup**

1 **tablespoon beef bouillon granules**

2 **teaspoons Worcestershire sauce**

2 **teaspoons balsamic vinegar**

⅛ **teaspoon red pepper flakes**

¼ **cup chopped fresh parsley**

1. Brown beef in large skillet over medium-high heat 6 to 8 minutes, stirring to break up meat. Drain fat. Remove to plate.

2. Heat oil in same skillet. Add cabbage and bell pepper; cook and stir 4 minutes or until cabbage is wilted. Add beef, water, tomatoes, mixed vegetables, ketchup, bouillon, Worcestershire sauce, vinegar and red pepper flakes; bring to a boil. Reduce heat; cover and simmer 20 minutes.

3. Remove from heat; let stand 5 minutes. Stir in parsley just before serving.

COUNTRY CHICKEN CHOWDER

MAKES 4 SERVINGS

1 pound chicken tenders
2 tablespoons butter or margarine
1 small onion, chopped
1 stalk celery, sliced
1 small carrot, sliced

1 can (10¾ ounces) condensed cream of potato soup, undiluted
1 cup milk
1 cup frozen corn
½ teaspoon dried dill weed

1. Cut chicken tenders into ½-inch pieces.

2. Melt butter in large saucepan or Dutch oven over medium-high heat. Add chicken; cook and stir 5 minutes.

3. Add onion, celery and carrot; cook and stir 3 minutes. Stir in soup, milk, corn and dill weed; reduce heat to low. Cook about 8 minutes or until corn is tender and chowder is heated through. Add salt and pepper to taste.

TIP: For a special touch, garnish soup with croutons and fresh dill. For a hearty winter meal, serve the chowder in hollowed-out toasted French rolls or small round sourdough loaves.

HEARTY MUSHROOM BARLEY SOUP

MAKES 4 SERVINGS

1 teaspoon extra virgin olive oil

2 cups chopped onions

1 cup thinly sliced carrots

2 cans (about 14 ounces each) fat-free reduced-sodium chicken broth

12 ounces sliced mushrooms

1 can (10¾ ounces) 98% fat-free cream of mushroom soup, undiluted

½ cup uncooked quick-cooking barley

1 teaspoon reduced-sodium Worcestershire sauce

½ teaspoon dried thyme

¼ cup finely chopped green onions

¼ teaspoon salt

¼ teaspoon black pepper

1. Coat Dutch oven or large saucepan with nonstick cooking spray; heat over medium-high heat until hot. Add oil and tilt pan to coat bottom of pan. Add onions; cook and stir 8 minutes or until onions just begin to turn golden. Add carrots; cook and stir 2 minutes.

2. Add broth, mushrooms, soup, barley, Worcestershire sauce and thyme; bring to a boil over high heat. Reduce heat; cover and simmer 15 minutes, stirring occasionally. Stir in green onions, salt and pepper.

STOVETOP DINNERS

SKILLET LASAGNA WITH VEGETABLES

MAKES 6 SERVINGS

½ pound hot Italian turkey sausage, casings removed

½ pound 93% lean ground turkey

2 stalks celery, sliced

⅓ cup chopped onion

2 cups marinara sauce

1⅓ cups water

4 ounces uncooked bowtie (farfalle) pasta

1 medium zucchini, halved lengthwise, then cut crosswise into ½-inch slices (2 cups)

¾ cup chopped green or yellow bell pepper

½ cup (2 ounces) shredded part-skim mozzarella cheese

½ cup reduced-fat ricotta cheese

2 tablespoons finely grated Parmesan cheese

1. Heat large skillet over medium-high heat. Add sausage, ground turkey, celery and onion; cook and stir 6 to 8 minutes or until turkey is no longer pink. Stir in marinara sauce and water; bring to a boil. Stir in pasta. Reduce heat to medium-low; cover and simmer 12 minutes.

2. Stir in zucchini and bell pepper; cover and simmer 2 minutes. Uncover and simmer 4 to 6 minutes or until vegetables are crisp-tender.

3. Sprinkle with mozzarella. Combine ricotta and Parmesan in small bowl; stir to blend. Drop by rounded teaspoonfuls on top of mixture in skillet. Remove from heat; cover and let stand 10 minutes.

LEMONY SEASONED TILAPIA FILLETS

2 tablespoons butter, melted

2 teaspoons dried oregano

1 teaspoon grated lemon peel

1 tablespoon lemon juice

Salt and black pepper, to taste

4 tilapia fillets (about 1 pound)

2 tablespoons olive oil

1. Combine butter, oregano, lemon peel, lemon juice, salt and pepper in small bowl. Brush both sides of tilapia with butter mixture.

2. Heat oil in large skillet over medium-high heat. Cook tilapia 4 to 5 minutes; turn. Cook 4 to 5 minutes or until fish begins to flake when tested with fork.

CHICKEN BACON QUESADILLAS

MAKES 4 SERVINGS

---

4 teaspoons vegetable oil, divided

4 (8-inch) flour tortillas

1 cup (4 ounces) shredded Colby-Jack cheese

2 cups coarsely chopped cooked chicken

4 slices bacon, crisp-cooked and coarsely chopped

½ cup pico de gallo, plus additional for serving

Sour cream and guacamole (optional)

---

1. Heat large nonstick skillet over medium heat; brush with 1 teaspoon oil. Place one tortilla in skillet; sprinkle with ¼ cup cheese. Spread ½ cup chicken over one half of tortilla; top with one fourth of bacon and 2 tablespoons pico de gallo.

2. Cook 1 to 2 minutes or until cheese is melted and bottom of tortilla is lightly browned. Fold tortilla over filling, pressing with spatula. Remove to cutting board; cool slightly. Cut into wedges. Repeat with remaining ingredients. Serve with additional pico de gallo, sour cream and guacamole, if desired.

JAMBALAYA PASTA

MAKES 4 SERVINGS

---

1 pound boneless skinless chicken breasts, cut into 1-inch pieces

2 tablespoons plus 1 teaspoon Cajun spice blend, divided

1 tablespoon vegetable oil

8 ounces bell peppers (red, yellow, green or a combination), cut into ¼-inch strips

½ medium red onion, cut into ¼-inch strips

6 ounces medium raw shrimp, peeled and deveined

2 cloves garlic, minced

1 teaspoon salt

¼ teaspoon black pepper

1½ pounds plum tomatoes (about 6), cut into ½-inch pieces

1 cup chicken broth

1 package (16 ounces) fresh or dried linguini, cooked and drained

Chopped fresh parsley

---

1. Combine chicken and 2 tablespoons Cajun seasoning in medium bowl; toss to coat. Heat oil in large skillet over medium-high heat. Add chicken; cook and stir 3 minutes.

2. Add bell peppers and onion; cook and stir 3 minutes. Add shrimp, garlic, remaining 1 teaspoon Cajun seasoning, salt and black pepper; cook and stir 1 minute.

3. Stir in tomatoes and broth; bring to a boil. Reduce heat to medium-low; cook 3 minutes or until shrimp are pink and opaque. Serve over hot pasta; sprinkle with parsley.

BARBECUE BEEF SANDWICHES

MAKES 4 SERVINGS

2½ **pounds boneless beef chuck roast**

2 **tablespoons Southwest seasoning**

1 **tablespoon vegetable oil**

1¼ **cups beef broth**

2½ **cups barbecue sauce, divided**

4 **sandwich or pretzel buns, split**

1⅓ **cups prepared coleslaw* (preferably vinegar based)**

*Vinegar-based coleslaws provide a perfect complement to the rich beef; they can often be found at the salad bar or prepared foods section of large supermarkets.

---

1. Sprinkle both sides of beef with Southwest seasoning. Heat oil in Dutch oven over medium-high heat. Add beef; cook about 6 minutes per side or until browned. Remove to plate.

2. Add broth to Dutch oven; cook 2 minutes, scraping up browned bits from bottom of Dutch oven. Stir in 2 cups barbecue sauce; bring to a boil. Return beef to Dutch oven; turn to coat.

3. Reduce heat to low; cover and cook 3 to 3½ hours or until beef is fork-tender, turning beef halfway through cooking time.

4. Remove beef to large bowl; let stand until cool enough to handle. Meanwhile, cook sauce remaining in Dutch oven over high heat about 10 minutes or until reduced and slightly thickened.

5. Shred beef into bite-size pieces. Stir in 1 cup reduced cooking sauce and ¼ cup barbecue sauce. Add remaining ¼ cup barbecue sauce, if desired. Fill buns with beef mixture; top with coleslaw.

SHRIMP CAPRESE PASTA

MAKES 4 SERVINGS

3 cups cooked whole wheat penne pasta, cooked without salt and reserving ½ cup cooking water

2 teaspoons olive oil

2 cups coarsely chopped grape tomatoes

4 tablespoons chopped fresh basil, divided

1 tablespoon balsamic vinegar

2 cloves garlic, minced

¼ teaspoon salt

⅛ teaspoon red pepper flakes

8 ounces medium raw shrimp, peeled and deveined (with tails on)

1 cup grape tomatoes, halved

2 ounces fresh mozzarella cheese pearls

1. Heat oil in large skillet over medium heat. Add 2 cups chopped tomatoes, reserved ½ cup pasta water, 2 tablespoons basil, vinegar, garlic, salt and red pepper flakes. Cook and stir 10 minutes or until tomatoes begin to soften.

2. Add shrimp and 1 cup halved tomatoes to skillet; cook and stir 5 minutes or until shrimp turn pink and opaque. Add pasta; cook until heated through.

3. Divide mixture evenly among four bowls. Top evenly with cheese and remaining 2 tablespoons basil.

BRATWURST SKILLET

MAKES 4 SERVINGS

---

1 pound bratwurst links, cut into ½-inch slices

1½ cups sliced onions

1½ cups green bell pepper strips

1½ cups red bell pepper strips

1 teaspoon paprika

1 teaspoon caraway seeds

---

1. Heat large skillet over medium heat. Add bratwurst; cover and cook about 5 minutes or until browned and no longer pink in center. Remove bratwurst to plate. Cover and keep warm.

2. Drain all but 1 tablespoon drippings from skillet. Add onions, bell peppers, paprika and caraway seeds. Cook and stir about 5 minutes or until vegetables are tender.

3. Combine bratwurst and vegetables. Serve immediately.

SERVING SUGGESTION: For a special touch, garnish dish with cherry tomato halves and celery leaves.

TIP: To make this even speedier, purchase a packaged stir-fry pepper and onion mix and use in place of the bell peppers and onions.

ZESTY SKILLET PORK CHOPS

MAKES 4 SERVINGS

- 1 teaspoon chili powder
- ½ teaspoon salt, divided
- 4 lean boneless pork chops (about 1¼ pounds), well trimmed
- 2 cups diced tomatoes
- 1 cup chopped green, red or yellow bell pepper
- ¾ cup thinly sliced celery
- ½ cup chopped onion
- 1 teaspoon dried thyme
- 1 tablespoon hot pepper sauce
- 2 tablespoons finely chopped fresh parsley

---

1. Rub chili powder and ¼ teaspoon salt evenly over one side of pork chops.

2. Combine tomatoes, bell peppers, celery, onion, thyme and hot pepper sauce in medium bowl; mix well.

3. Lightly spray large nonstick skillet with nonstick cooking spray; heat over medium-high heat. Add pork, seasoned side down; cook 1 minute. Turn pork. Top with tomato mixture; bring to a boil. Reduce heat to low. Cover; cook 25 minutes or until pork is tender and tomato mixture has thickened.

4. Remove pork to serving plates. Bring tomato mixture to a boil over high heat; cook 2 minutes or until most liquid has evaporated. Remove from heat; stir in parsley and remaining ¼ teaspoon salt. Spoon sauce over pork.

CHICKEN SCARPIELLO

MAKES 6 SERVINGS

3 tablespoons extra virgin olive oil, divided

1 pound spicy Italian sausage, cut into 1-inch pieces

1 whole chicken (about 3 pounds), cut into 10 pieces*

1 teaspoon salt, divided

1 large onion, chopped

2 red, yellow or orange bell peppers, cut into ¼-inch strips

3 cloves garlic, minced

½ cup dry white wine (such as sauvignon blanc)

½ cup chicken broth

½ cup coarsely chopped seeded hot cherry peppers

½ cup liquid from cherry pepper jar

1 teaspoon dried oregano

Additional salt and black pepper

¼ cup chopped fresh Italian parsley

*Or purchase 2 bone-in chicken leg quarters and 2 chicken breasts; separate drumsticks and thighs and cut breasts in half.

1. Heat 1 tablespoon oil in large skillet over medium-high heat. Add sausage; cook about 10 minutes or until well browned on all sides, stirring occasionally. Remove sausage from skillet; set aside.

2. Heat 1 tablespoon oil in same skillet. Sprinkle chicken with ½ teaspoon salt; arrange skin side down in single layer in skillet (cook in batches, if necessary). Cook about 6 minutes per side or until browned. Remove chicken from skillet; set aside. Drain oil from skillet.

3. Heat remaining 1 tablespoon oil in skillet. Add onion and ½ teaspoon salt; cook and stir 2 minutes or until onion is softened, scraping up browned bits from bottom of skillet. Add bell peppers and garlic; cook and stir 5 minutes. Stir in wine; cook until liquid is reduced by half. Stir in broth, cherry peppers, cherry pepper liquid and oregano. Season with additional salt and black pepper; bring to a simmer.

4. Return sausage and chicken along with any accumulated juices to skillet. Partially cover skillet; simmer 10 minutes. Uncover; simmer 15 minutes or until chicken is cooked through (165°F). Sprinkle with parsley.

TIP: If too much liquid remains in the skillet when the chicken is cooked through, remove the chicken and sausage and continue simmering the sauce to reduce it slightly.

NOODLES WITH BABY SHRIMP

MAKES 4 TO 6 SERVINGS

- **1 package (3¾ ounces) cellophane noodles**
- **3 green onions**
- **1 tablespoon vegetable oil**
- **1 package (16 ounces) frozen mixed vegetables (such as cauliflower, broccoli and carrots)**

- **1 cup vegetable broth**
- **8 ounces cooked frozen baby shrimp**
- **1 tablespoon soy sauce**
- **2 teaspoons dark sesame oil**
- **¼ teaspoon black pepper**

---

1. Place noodles in large bowl. Cover with boiling water; let stand 10 to 15 minutes or just until softened. Drain noodles. Cut noodles into 5- or 6-inch pieces; set aside. Cut green onions into 1-inch pieces.

2. Heat wok or large skillet over high heat about 1 minute or until hot. Drizzle vegetable oil into wok; heat 30 seconds. Add green onions; stir-fry 1 minute. Add mixed vegetables; stir-fry 2 minutes. Add broth; bring to a boil. Reduce heat to low; cover and cook 5 minutes or until vegetables are crisp-tender.

3. Add shrimp to wok; cook just until thawed. Stir in noodles, soy sauce, sesame oil and pepper; stir-fry until heated through.

TIP: Cellophane noodles are also called bean thread noodles or glass noodles. They are sold in packages of 6 to 8 tangled bunches in the Asian section of the supermarket.

MOZZARELLA-PEPPER SAUSAGE SKILLET

MAKES 4 SERVINGS

- 1 pound mild Italian sausage, casings removed
- 1 tablespoon olive oil
- 1 package (8 ounces) sliced mushrooms
- 1 zucchini, thinly sliced
- ¾ cup finely chopped onion
- 1 tablespoon dried basil

- 1 can (8 ounces) tomato sauce
- ½ cup plain dry bread crumbs
- ¼ teaspoon salt
- 1 red bell pepper, cut into strips
- 1 green bell pepper, cut into strips
- 1½ cups (6 ounces) shredded mozzarella cheese

---

1. Brown sausage in large nonstick skillet over medium-high heat 6 to 8 minutes, stirring to break up meat. Remove sausage to plate; drain fat.

2. Add oil to same skillet. Add mushrooms, zucchini, onion and basil; cook and stir 5 minutes or until zucchini is tender.

3. Return sausage to skillet. Add tomato sauce, bread crumbs and salt; mix well. Top mixture with bell peppers. Cover; simmer 25 minutes or until bell peppers are tender. Remove from heat. Sprinkle with cheese. Cover; let stand until cheese is melted.

EASY TERIYAKI CHICKEN SKILLET

MAKES 2 TO 3 SERVINGS

¼ cup water

¼ cup teriyaki sauce

1 tablespoon honey

1 teaspoon minced fresh ginger

½ teaspoon cornstarch

2 tablespoons vegetable oil

¼ pound fresh snow peas, trimmed and cut in half (about 1 cup)

1 cup shredded carrots *or* 1 large carrot, cut into thin strips

1 teaspoon minced garlic

1 package (about 8 ounces) refrigerated fully cooked chicken strips, cut into ½-inch pieces

4 ounces regular or whole wheat angel hair pasta, cooked and drained

1 teaspoon sesame seeds (optional)

1. Combine water, teriyaki sauce, honey, ginger and cornstarch in small bowl; set aside.

2. Heat oil in large skillet over medium heat. Add snow peas, carrots and garlic. Cook and stir 4 minutes or until crisp-tender.

3. Add chicken, pasta and teriyaki mixture. Cook and stir 2 to 4 minutes or until sauce is slightly thickened and mixture is heated through. Garnish with sesame seeds.

SUBSTITUTION: Two cups chopped cooked chicken can be substituted for chicken strips.

MEAT LOAF ROUNDS WITH SKILLET RICE

MAKES 4 SERVINGS

---

12 ounces extra-lean ground beef

4 ounces turkey sausage or 50%-less-fat pork bulk sausage

⅔ cup picante sauce, divided

2 large egg whites

½ cup quick-cooking oats

2 tablespoons ketchup

¼ teaspoon Worcestershire sauce

2 cups cooked brown rice

---

1. Mix together beef, sausage, ⅓ cup picante sauce, egg whites and oats in medium bowl. Shape into four (½-inch-thick) patties. Heat large nonstick skillet over medium heat until hot. Coat skillet with nonstick cooking spray. Add patties. Cook 5 minutes.

2. Meanwhile, mix together 2 tablespoons picante sauce, ketchup and Worcestershire sauce in small bowl. Turn patties. Spoon 1 tablespoon picante mixture on each patty. Reduce heat to medium-low. Cover. Cook 16 minutes or until no longer pink in centers.

3. Transfer patties to plate. Combine rice and remaining picante sauce in skillet. Stir, scraping bottom and sides of skillet. Place patties on rice mixture. Simmer 3 minutes.

NOTE: Quick-cooking oats and old-fashioned oats are essentially the same; the quick-cooking oats cook faster because they have been cut and rolled into thinner flakes. However, you can use old-fashioned oats if you prefer their texture in recipes.

BROCCOLI, TURKEY AND NOODLE SKILLET

MAKES 4 SERVINGS

---

1 tablespoon butter

1 red or green bell pepper, chopped

1 cup frozen chopped broccoli, thawed

¼ teaspoon black pepper

1½ cups chicken broth

½ cup milk or half-and-half

2 cups diced cooked turkey breast

1 package (about 4 ounces) chicken and broccoli pasta mix

¼ cup sour cream

---

1. Melt butter in large skillet over medium-high heat. Add bell pepper, broccoli and black pepper; cook and stir 5 minutes or until bell pepper is crisp-tender. Add broth and milk; bring to a boil. Stir in turkey and pasta mix.

2. Reduce heat to low. Cook 8 to 10 minutes or until noodles are tender. Remove from heat. Stir in sour cream. Let stand, uncovered, 5 minutes or until sauce thickens.

CHICKEN AND HERB STEW

MAKES 4 SERVINGS

½ cup all-purpose flour

½ teaspoon salt

¼ teaspoon black pepper

¼ teaspoon paprika

4 chicken drumsticks

4 chicken thighs

2 tablespoons olive oil

12 ounces unpeeled new red potatoes, quartered

2 carrots, quartered lengthwise, then cut crosswise into 3-inch pieces

1 green bell pepper, cut into thin strips

¾ cup chopped onion

2 cloves garlic, minced

1¾ cups water

¼ cup dry white wine

2 cubes chicken bouillon

1 tablespoon chopped fresh oregano

1 teaspoon chopped fresh rosemary leaves

2 tablespoons chopped fresh Italian parsley (optional)

1. Combine flour, salt, black pepper and paprika in shallow plate; stir until well blended. Coat chicken with flour mixture; shake off excess.

2. Heat oil in large skillet over medium-high heat. Add chicken; cook 10 minutes or until browned on both sides, turning once. Remove to plate.

3. Add potatoes, carrots, bell pepper, onion and garlic to skillet; cook 6 minutes or until vegetables are lightly browned, stirring occasionally. Add water, wine and bouillon; cook 1 minute, scraping up browned bits from bottom of skillet. Stir in oregano and rosemary.

4. Place chicken on top of vegetable mixture, turning several times to coat. Cover and simmer 45 to 50 minutes or until chicken is cooked through (165°F), turning occasionally. Garnish with parsley.

SHRIMP AND SAUSAGE SKILLET DINNER

MAKES 4 SERVINGS

---

1 red bell pepper

1 teaspoon olive oil

1 onion, chopped

1 clove garlic, minced

2 (2-ounce) chicken chorizo sausage links, thinly sliced

½ cup low-sodium chicken broth

6 ounces large raw shrimp, peeled, deveined and cut into bite-size pieces

1 cup frozen green peas

1 cup cooked brown rice

¼ teaspoon salt

¼ teaspoon black pepper

¼ teaspoon smoked paprika

---

1. Place bell pepper on rack in broiler pan 3 to 5 inches from heat source or hold over open gas flame on long-handled metal fork. Turn bell pepper often until blistered and charred on all sides. Transfer to food storage bag; seal bag and let stand 15 to 20 minutes to loosen skin. Remove loosened skin with paring knife. Cut off top and scrape out seeds; discard. Chop; set aside.

2. Heat oil in large nonstick skillet over medium-high heat. Add onion and garlic; cook and stir 3 minutes. Add sausage; cook and stir 2 minutes or until browned. Pour in broth, stirring to scrape up browned bits.

3. Stir shrimp, bell pepper, peas, rice, salt, black pepper and paprika into skillet. Reduce heat to low; cover and simmer 10 minutes.

BEEF AND VEGETABLE RAGOÛT

MAKES 6 SERVINGS

1 cup coarsely chopped onion

4 cloves garlic, minced

1¼ pounds boneless beef top round steak, trimmed and cut into 1-inch cubes

All-purpose flour

2 cans (about 14 ounces each) fat-free reduced-sodium beef broth*

2 tablespoons tomato paste

1 tablespoon Worcestershire sauce

2 teaspoons horseradish mustard

2 teaspoons dried oregano leaves, crushed

2 teaspoons dried thyme leaves, crushed

¼ teaspoon ground allspice

½ teaspoon salt

½ teaspoon black pepper

8 ounces baby carrots

2 cups medium whole mushrooms

4 medium plum tomatoes, cut into wedges, seeded

3 cups cooked no-yolk noodles

*To defat beef broth, skim fat from surface of broth with spoon. Or, place can of broth in refrigerator at least 2 hours ahead of time. Before using, remove fat that has hardened on surface of broth.

1. Coat Dutch oven or large saucepan with olive oil cooking spray; heat over medium heat. Add onion and garlic; cook and stir 3 to 5 minutes or until onion is softened.

2. Coat beef lightly with flour. Add to Dutch oven; cook and stir about 10 minutes or until browned on all sides.

3. Add beef broth, tomato paste, Worcestershire sauce, mustard, oregano, thyme, allspice, salt and pepper; bring to a boil over high heat. Reduce heat to low. Simmer, covered, about 1½ hours, adding carrots, mushrooms and tomatoes during last 45 minutes of cooking time. Serve over noodles.

MUSHROOM & CHICKEN SKILLET

MAKES 4 SERVINGS

---

1 pound boneless skinless chicken breasts, cut into bite-size pieces

1 can (about 14 ounces) fat-free chicken broth

¼ cup hot water

½ teaspoon dried thyme

2 cups uncooked instant rice

8 ounces mushrooms, thinly sliced

1 can (10¾ ounces) 98% fat-free cream of celery soup, undiluted

Chopped fresh parsley

---

1. Cook chicken in broth and water in large nonstick skillet until mixture comes to a full boil. Stir in thyme and rice. Place mushrooms on top. (Do not stir mushrooms into rice.) Cover skillet; turn off heat and let stand 5 minutes.

2. Stir in soup; cook over low heat 5 minutes or until heated through. Sprinkle with parsley.

TIP: Serve with mixed greens salad and sliced fresh strawberries.

GREEK-STYLE SALMON

MAKES 4 SERVINGS

1½ teaspoons olive oil

1¾ cups diced tomatoes, drained

6 pitted black olives, coarsely chopped

4 pitted green olives, coarsely chopped

3 tablespoons lemon juice

2 tablespoons chopped fresh Italian parsley

1 tablespoon capers, rinsed and drained

2 medium cloves garlic, thinly sliced

¼ teaspoon black pepper

1 pound salmon fillets

1. Heat oil in large skillet over medium heat. Add tomatoes, olives, lemon juice, parsley, capers, garlic and pepper; bring to a simmer, stirring frequently. Cook 5 minutes or until reduced by about one third, stirring occasionally.

2. Rinse salmon and pat dry with paper towels. Push sauce to one side of skillet. Add salmon; spoon sauce over salmon. Cover; cook 10 to 15 minutes or until salmon begins to flake when tested with fork.

SKILLET BEEF AND NOODLES

MAKES 6 SERVINGS

---

1 beef top sirloin steak (about ¾ pound)

1 can (10¾ ounces) condensed cream of mushroom soup, undiluted

¾ cup milk

½ cup sour cream

½ teaspoon salt (optional)

½ teaspoon black pepper

1 tablespoon margarine

1 can (about 14 ounces) pearl onions, drained or 2 cups thinly sliced onions

1 clove garlic, minced

1 teaspoon sugar

1 tablespoon white wine vinegar

1½ cups sliced mushrooms

4 cups hot cooked egg noodles

1 tablespoon minced fresh parsley

---

1. Cut beef lengthwise in half, then crosswise into thin strips. Blend soup, milk, sour cream, salt, if desired, and pepper in small bowl; set aside.

2. Melt margarine in large nonstick skillet over medium heat. Add onions and garlic; cook and stir until light brown. Add sugar; cook until golden brown, stirring constantly. Stir in vinegar; cook 1 minute. Remove from skillet; set aside.

3. Add mushrooms to same skillet; cook and stir until light brown. Remove from skillet; set aside. Increase heat to high. Add beef; stir-fry until browned. Remove from skillet; drain fat.

4. Add soup mixture to same skillet; cook over low heat until heated through. Stir in onions, mushrooms and beef; cook 2 minutes. (Do not boil.) Serve over noodles. Garnish with parsley.

RAMEN HASH

MAKES 6 SERVINGS

---

1 package (3 ounces) chicken-flavored ramen noodles, crumbled

2½ cups frozen country-style hash brown potatoes

½ cup finely chopped green onions or chopped fresh cilantro, divided

2 large eggs, beaten

1 teaspoon hot pepper sauce

½ teaspoon garlic powder

¼ teaspoon black pepper

1 tablespoon vegetable oil

1 can (15 ounces) chili with meat and beans

¾ cup (about 3 ounces) shredded Cheddar cheese

¾ cup sour cream (optional)

---

1. Prepare noodles according to package directions using large nonstick skillet. Rinse and drain under cool running water. Shake off excess liquid.

2. Transfer noodles to medium bowl; add hash browns, ramen seasoning packet, ¼ cup green onions, eggs, hot pepper sauce, garlic powder and black pepper. Stir until well blended.

3. Wipe skillet with paper towel. Heat oil in skillet over medium-high heat. Add noodle mixture and spread evenly over bottom of skillet. Cook 3 minutes, do not stir. (This will create browning and crusting.) After 3 minutes, cook and stir until egg is cooked through and hash browns are golden brown, about 6 to 8 minutes more.

4. Meanwhile, place chili in microwavable bowl; cover. Microwave on HIGH 1 to 2 minutes or until heated through. Top noodle mixture with chili, cheese and remaining green onions. Serve topped with sour cream, if desired.

CHICKEN SAUSAGE AND TWO-GRAIN SKILLET CASSEROLE

MAKES 4 SERVINGS

---

1 package (12 ounces) fully cooked chicken apple sausage links, sliced

1 can (about 14 ounces) reduced-sodium chicken broth

1 cup uncooked instant brown rice

½ cup uncooked quinoa, preferably the white grain variety

1 red bell pepper, cut into thin strips

1 stalk celery, sliced diagonally

1½ teaspoons curry powder or 1 teaspoon ground turmeric

½ cup thawed frozen peas

¼ cup finely chopped green onions (optional)

---

1. Heat large skillet coated with nonstick cooking spray over medium-high heat; cook sausage 3 minutes or until edges are browned, stirring occasionally.

2. Stir in broth, rice, quinoa, bell pepper, celery and curry powder; bring to a boil. Reduce heat to low; cover and simmer 12 minutes or until liquid is absorbed.

3. Remove from heat. Stir in peas. Let stand 5 minutes to continue cooking without drying out. Sprinkle with green onions, if desired.

FRENCH DIP SANDWICHES

MAKES 6 SERVINGS

3 pounds boneless beef chuck roast

½ teaspoon salt

½ teaspoon black pepper

1 tablespoon olive oil

2 large onions, cut into halves, then cut into ¼-inch slices

2¼ cups reduced-sodium beef broth, divided

3 tablespoons Worcestershire sauce

6 hoagie rolls, split and heated

12 slices provolone cheese

1. Season beef with salt and pepper. Heat oil in Dutch oven or large saucepan over medium-high heat. Add beef; cook about 6 minutes per side or until browned. Remove to plate.

2. Add onions and ¼ cup broth to Dutch oven; cook 8 minutes or until golden brown, stirring occasionally and scraping up browned bits from bottom of pan. Remove half of onions to small bowl; set aside. Stir in remaining 2 cups broth and Worcestershire sauce; mix well. Return beef to Dutch oven. Reduce heat to low; cover and cook 3 to 3½ hours or until beef is fork-tender.

3. Remove beef to large bowl; let stand until cool enough to handle. Shred into bite-size pieces. Add ⅔ cup cooking liquid; toss to coat. Pour remaining cooking liquid into small bowl for serving.

4. Place warmed rolls cut side up on serving plate. Top bottom of rolls with cheese, beef and reserved onions. Serve with warm au jus for dipping.

LENTILS WITH PASTA

MAKES 6 TO 8 SERVINGS

1 cup dried lentils

1 cup dried split peas

1 tablespoon olive oil

1 onion, chopped

2 tablespoons tomato paste

2 cloves garlic, minced

1 teaspoon salt

¼ teaspoon black pepper

1 can (about 14 ounces) diced tomatoes

3 cups water

12 ounces short pasta (elbow macaroni, small shells, ditalini or similar), cooked according to package directions for al dente and drained

Shredded Romano or Parmesan cheese (optional)

1. Place lentils and split peas in medium bowl; cover with water. Let stand at least 10 minutes.

2. Heat oil in large saucepan or Dutch oven over medium heat. Add onion; cook and stir 5 minutes or until onion is lightly browned. Add tomato paste, garlic, salt and pepper; cook and stir 1 minute. Add tomatoes and 3 cups water; bring to a boil.

3. Drain lentils and split peas and add to saucepan. Reduce heat to medium-low; cover and simmer about 40 minutes or until lentils and split peas are tender.

4. Add pasta to lentil mixture; mix well. Serve with Romano cheese, if desired.

SKILLET MAC & CHEESE

MAKES 6 SERVINGS

8 ounces thick-cut bacon, cut into ½-inch pieces, cooked crisp and drained, reserving drippings

¼ cup finely chopped onion

¼ cup all-purpose flour

3½ cups whole milk

1 cup (4 ounces) shredded white Cheddar cheese

1 cup (4 ounces) shredded fontina cheese

1 cup (4 ounces) shredded Gruyère cheese

¾ cup grated Parmesan cheese, divided

½ teaspoon salt

½ teaspoon dry mustard

¼ teaspoon ground red pepper

¼ teaspoon black pepper

8 cups cavatappi or rotini pasta, cooked al dente and drained

¼ cup panko bread crumbs

1. Preheat oven to 400°F.

2. Heat 4 tablespoons bacon drippings in large ovenproof skillet over medium-high heat. Add onion; cook and stir 4 minutes or until translucent. Add flour; cook and stir 5 minutes. Slowly add milk over medium-low heat, stirring constantly. Stir in Cheddar, fontina, Gruyère, ½ cup Parmesan, salt, mustard, red pepper and black pepper until smooth and well blended. Add cooked pasta; stir gently until coated. Stir in bacon.

3. Combine panko and remaining ¼ cup Parmesan in small bowl; sprinkle over pasta. Bake 30 minutes or until top is golden brown.

CHICKEN BOWTIE PARTY

MAKES 4 SERVINGS

6 slices bacon, chopped

12 ounces boneless skinless chicken breasts, cut into 2×½-inch strips*

⅓ cup chopped red onion

1 teaspoon minced garlic

2 plum tomatoes, diced (about ½ cup)

1 cup whipping cream

¼ cup shredded Asiago cheese, plus additional for garnish

1 package (10 to 12 ounces) bowtie (farfalle) pasta, cooked according to package directions for al dente and drained

1 jar (15 ounces) Alfredo sauce
   Finely chopped fresh parsley (optional)

Or substitute 12 ounces grilled chicken breast strips; add to skillet with tomatoes in step 2.

1. Cook bacon in large skillet over medium-high heat until cooked through. (Bacon should still be chewy, not quite crisp.) Remove to paper towel-lined plate. Drain all but 1 tablespoon drippings from skillet.

2. Add chicken to skillet; cook about 4 minutes or until chicken begins to brown, turning occasionally. Add onion and garlic; cook and stir 2 minutes. Add tomatoes and bacon; cook and stir 1 minute. Stir in cream and ¼ cup cheese; cook about 4 minutes or until liquid is slightly reduced.

3. Add pasta and Alfredo sauce to chicken mixture in skillet; stir gently to coat. Cook over medium heat until heated through, stirring occasionally. Garnish with parsley and additional cheese.

OVEN BAKES

LEMON GARLIC ROAST CHICKEN

MAKES 4 SERVINGS

4 **sprigs fresh rosemary, divided**
6 **cloves garlic, divided**
1 **lemon**
2 **tablespoons butter, softened**
2 **teaspoons salt, divided**

2 **large russet potatoes, cut into ¾-inch pieces**
2 **onions, cut into 1-inch pieces**
2 **tablespoons olive oil**
½ **teaspoon black pepper**
1 **whole chicken (3 to 4 pounds)**

1. Preheat oven to 400°F. Finely chop 2 sprigs rosemary (about 2 tablespoons). Mince 3 cloves garlic. Grate peel from lemon. Combine butter, chopped rosemary, minced garlic, lemon peel and ½ teaspoon salt in small bowl; mix well. Set aside while preparing vegetables.

2. Combine potatoes, onions, oil, 1 teaspoon salt and ½ teaspoon pepper in medium bowl; toss to coat. Spread mixture in single layer in large (12-inch) cast iron skillet.

3. Smash remaining 3 cloves garlic. Cut lemon into quarters. Season cavity of chicken with remaining ½ teaspoon salt. Place garlic, lemon quarters and remaining 2 sprigs rosemary in cavity; tie legs with kitchen string, if desired. Place chicken on top of vegetables in skillet; spread butter mixture over chicken.

4. Roast about 1 hour or until chicken is cooked through (165°F) and potatoes are tender. Let stand 10 minutes before carving. Sprinkle with additional salt and pepper to taste.

SAUSAGE, POTATO AND APPLE BAKE

MAKES 6 SERVINGS

3 tablespoons packed brown sugar

1 tablespoon dried thyme

1 tablespoon dried oregano

¼ cup dry white wine or apple cider

2 tablespoons cider vinegar

2 sweet potatoes (1½ to 2 pounds), peeled

2 apples, such as Fuji or McIntosh, peeled

1 white onion

1 red bell pepper

1 yellow bell pepper

½ cup golden raisins

1½ pounds smoked sausage, such as kielbasa or Polish sausage, sliced diagonally into ¼-inch pieces

1. Preheat oven to 450°F. Spray 13×9-inch baking dish or 2-quart casserole with nonstick cooking spray.

2. Combine brown sugar, thyme and oregano in large bowl. Stir in white wine and vinegar until brown sugar is dissolved.

3. Spiral sweet potatoes, apples and onion with thick spiral blade. Spiral bell peppers with spiral slicing blade.* Cut vegetables into desired lengths. Add vegetables and raisins to brown sugar mixture; toss to coat.

4. Transfer vegetables to prepared baking dish using tongs or slotted spoon. Mix in sausage; drizzle with remaining brown sugar mixture. Bake 20 minutes or until vegetables are tender.

*If you don't have a spiralizer, cut the vegetables and apples into thin strips.

HONEY MUSTARD HERBED LAMB WITH VEGETABLES

MAKES 4 SERVINGS

---

3 tablespoons finely chopped fresh parsley

2 tablespoons minced fresh rosemary

2 cloves garlic, minced

1¼ teaspoons salt

½ teaspoon black pepper

¼ cup olive oil

2 tablespoons honey

2 tablespoons whole grain mustard

4 lamb shoulder chops (6 to 8 ounces each)

1 pound unpeeled small red potatoes, cut into halves (or quarters if large)

1 pound unpeeled small yellow potatoes, cut into halves (or quarters if large)

1½ pounds medium carrots, peeled, cut in half lengthwise then cut into 2-inch lengths

---

1. Preheat oven to 425°F. Combine parsley, rosemary, garlic, salt and pepper in small bowl; mix well. Stir in oil until well blended.

2. Remove half of mixture to large shallow dish; stir in honey and mustard. Add lamb chops to dish; turn to coat both sides with mustard mixture. Set aside to marinate while preparing vegetables.

3. Combine potatoes and carrots on baking sheet. Stir remaining half of oil mixture; drizzle over vegetables and toss to coat. Cover baking sheet with foil.

4. Roast 40 minutes. Uncover; stir vegetables and roast 10 minutes. Remove baking sheet from oven; *turn oven to broil.* Arrange lamb chops over vegetables.

5. Broil 6 minutes. Turn lamb; broil 6 minutes or until medium (140°F). (Cooking time may vary depending on how quickly oven reaches broiling temperature.)

SHEET PAN CHICKEN AND SAUSAGE SUPPER

MAKES ABOUT 6 SERVINGS

⅓ cup olive oil

2 tablespoons balsamic vinegar

1 teaspoon salt

1 teaspoon garlic powder

½ teaspoon black pepper

¼ teaspoon red pepper flakes

3 pounds bone-in chicken thighs and drumsticks

1 pound uncooked sweet Italian sausage (4 to 5 links), cut diagonally into 2-inch pieces

6 to 8 small red onions (about 1½ pounds), each cut into 6 wedges

3½ cups broccoli florets

---

1. Preheat oven to 425°F. Line baking sheet with foil, if desired.

2. Whisk oil, vinegar, salt, garlic powder, black pepper and red pepper flakes in small bowl until well blended. Combine chicken, sausage and onions on prepared baking sheet. Drizzle with oil mixture; toss until well coated. Spread into single layer (chicken thighs should be skin side up).

3. Bake 30 minutes. Add broccoli to baking sheet; stir to coat broccoli with pan juices and turn sausage. Bake 30 minutes or until broccoli is beginning to brown and chicken is cooked through (165°F).

GARLIC AND ONION SHEET PAN PIZZA

MAKES 16 SQUARES

---

2 teaspoons vegetable oil

1 head cauliflower (1½ pounds)

¾ cup almond flour

½ cup shredded Parmesan cheese

1½ cups (6 ounces) shredded mozzarella cheese, divided

1 teaspoon salt

1 clove garlic

½ teaspoon dried oregano

Black pepper

1 egg

1 cup prepared Indian butter chicken sauce*

½ sweet onion, halved and thinly sliced

1 tablespoon chopped garlic

Or stir ¼ cup whipping cream into 1 cup prepared marinara sauce in small bowl.

---

1. Preheat oven to 425°F. Grease baking sheet with oil.

2. Break cauliflower into florets. Working in batches, pulse cauliflower in food processor until finely chopped. Measure 4 cups; place in large bowl. Reserve remaining cauliflower for another use. Add flour, Parmesan cheese, ½ cup mozzarella cheese, 1 teaspoon salt, 1 clove garlic and oregano. Season with black pepper; mix well. Add egg; mix with hands until thoroughly blended. Turn out onto prepared sheet pan; pat into 11×14-inch rectangle. Bake 20 minutes.

3. Remove crust from oven. Spread sauce over crust to within ½ inch of edges. Sprinkle evenly with onion, chopped garlic and remaining 1 cup mozzarella cheese. Bake 7 to 10 minutes or until cheese is bubbly and browned in spots. Cut into squares to serve.

CHICKEN ZUCCHINI CASSEROLE

MAKES 8 SERVINGS

---

1 package (about 6 ounces) herb-flavored stuffing mix

½ cup (1 stick) butter, melted

2 cups cubed zucchini

1½ cups chopped cooked chicken

1 can (10¾ ounces) condensed cream of celery soup, undiluted

1 cup grated carrots

1 onion, chopped

½ cup sour cream

½ cup (2 ounces) shredded Cheddar cheese

---

1. Preheat oven to 350°F. Combine stuffing mix and butter in medium bowl; reserve 1 cup stuffing. Place remaining stuffing in 13×9-inch baking dish.

2. Combine zucchini, chicken, soup, carrots, onion and sour cream in large bowl; mix well. Pour over stuffing in baking dish; top with reserved 1 cup stuffing and cheese.

3. Bake 40 to 45 minutes or until heated through and cheese is melted.

CAULIFLOWER, SAUSAGE AND GOUDA SHEET PAN

MAKES 6 SERVINGS

- 1 package (16 ounces) white mushrooms, stemmed and halved
- 3 tablespoons olive oil, divided
- 1 teaspoon salt, divided
- 1 head cauliflower, separated into florets and thinly sliced
- ¼ teaspoon chipotle chili powder

- 1 package (about 13 ounces) smoked sausage, cut into ¼-inch slices
- 2 tablespoons peach or apricot preserves
- 1 tablespoon Dijon mustard
- ½ red onion, thinly sliced
- 6 ounces Gouda cheese, cubed

---

1. Preheat oven to 400°F.

2. Place mushrooms in medium bowl. Drizzle with 1 tablespoon oil and sprinkle with ½ teaspoon salt; toss to coat. Spread on baking sheet.

3. Place cauliflower, remaining 2 tablespoons oil, ½ teaspoon salt and chipotle chili powder in same bowl; toss to coat. Spread on sheet pan with mushrooms.

4. Combine sausage, preserves and mustard in same bowl; stir until well coated. Arrange sausage over vegetables; top with onion.

5. Bake 30 minutes. Remove from oven; place cheese cubes on top of cauliflower. Bake 5 minutes or until cheese is melted and cauliflower is tender.

SPATCHCOCK CHICKEN AND VEGETABLES

MAKES 4 SERVINGS

---

1 whole chicken (about 4 pounds)

6 tablespoons (¾ stick) butter, softened

2 tablespoons fresh thyme leaves

1 tablespoon honey

1 tablespoon Dijon mustard

1¼ teaspoons salt

½ teaspoon black pepper

12 (2-inch) unpeeled small red potatoes, halved

8 ounces parsnips, cut diagonally into 1½-inch pieces (cut in half lengthwise if very thick)

8 ounces carrots, cut diagonally into 1½-inch pieces

---

1. Position oven rack in lower third of oven. Preheat oven to 425°F. Line baking sheet with foil, if desired.

2. To spatchcock chicken, place breast side down on cutting board. Cut along both sides of backbone with poultry shears or kitchen scissors; remove and discard backbone. Turn chicken breast side up; press down firmly on breast until it cracks to flatten chicken. Place on prepared baking sheet.

3. Combine butter, thyme, honey, mustard, salt and pepper in small microwavable bowl; mix well. Rub 1 tablespoon mixture under skin of chicken breast. Rub 1 tablespoon mixture all over chicken skin.

4. Combine potatoes, parsnips and carrots in large bowl. Melt remaining butter mixture in microwave oven; pour over vegetables and toss to coat. Arrange vegetables around chicken on baking sheet.

5. Roast 50 to 60 minutes or until chicken is cooked through (165°F), covering chicken loosely with foil after 30 minutes if skin is turning too dark. Remove chicken to clean cutting board; tent with foil and let stand 10 minutes before slicing. Serve with vegetables.

TUNA-MACARONI CASSEROLE

MAKES 6 SERVINGS

1 cup mayonnaise

1 cup (4 ounces) shredded Swiss cheese

½ cup milk

¼ cup chopped onion

¼ cup chopped red bell pepper

⅛ teaspoon black pepper

2 cans (about 6 ounces each) tuna, drained and flaked

1 package (about 10 ounces) frozen peas

2 cups shell pasta or elbow macaroni, cooked and drained

½ cup dry bread crumbs

2 tablespoons melted butter

Chopped fresh parsley (optional)

1. Preheat oven to 350°F.

2. Combine mayonnaise, cheese, milk, onion, bell pepper and black pepper in large bowl. Add tuna, peas and pasta; toss to coat well. Spoon into 2-quart casserole.

3. Mix bread crumbs with butter in small bowl; sprinkle over top of casserole. Bake 30 to 40 minutes or until heated through. Top with chopped parsley, if desired.

MOM'S BAKED MOSTACCIOLI

MAKES 8 SERVINGS

1 container (15 ounces) part-skim ricotta cheese

½ cup cholesterol-free egg substitute

¼ cup grated Parmesan cheese

Garlic powder

Black pepper

Italian seasoning

1 package (16 ounces) mostaccioli, cooked and drained

1 jar (26 ounces) prepared pasta sauce

1½ cups (6 ounces) shredded mozzarella cheese

1. Preheat oven to 350°F. Spray 13×9-inch casserole with nonstick cooking spray.

2. Combine ricotta cheese, egg substitute and Parmesan cheese in medium bowl. Season with garlic powder, pepper and Italian seasoning; mix well.

3. Place half of pasta and half the sauce in prepared casserole. Spread ricotta mixture evenly over pasta. Spoon remaining pasta and sauce over ricotta mixture. Top with mozzarella cheese.

4. Bake 30 minutes or until hot and bubbly.

SOUTHERN-STYLE CHICKEN AND GREENS
MAKES 4 TO 6 SERVINGS

1 teaspoon salt

1 teaspoon paprika

½ teaspoon black pepper

3½ pounds bone-in chicken pieces

4 thick slices smoked bacon (4 ounces), cut crosswise into ¼-inch strips

1 cup uncooked rice

1 can (about 14 ounces) stewed tomatoes, undrained

1¼ cups chicken broth

2 cups packed coarsely chopped fresh collard or mustard greens or kale (3 to 4 ounces)

1. Preheat oven to 350°F. Combine salt, paprika and pepper in small bowl; sprinkle over chicken.

2. Cook and stir bacon in Dutch oven over medium heat until crisp. Drain on paper towel-lined plate. Add chicken in batches to drippings in Dutch oven; cook 5 minutes per side or until browned. (Cook chicken in single layer; do not crowd pieces.) Remove to plate. Drain all but 1 tablespoon drippings from Dutch oven.

3. Add rice to drippings; cook and stir 1 minute. Add tomatoes with juice, broth, collard greens and half of bacon; bring to a boil over high heat. Remove from heat; arrange chicken over rice mixture.

4. Cover and bake about 40 minutes or until chicken is cooked through (165°F) and most of liquid is absorbed. Let stand 5 minutes before serving. Sprinkle with remaining bacon.

SERVING SUGGESTION: Serve with corn bread or corn muffins.

PORK TENDERLOIN WITH CABBAGE AND LEEKS

MAKES 4 SERVINGS

¼ cup olive oil, plus additional for pan

1 teaspoon salt

¾ teaspoon garlic powder

½ teaspoon dried thyme

½ teaspoon black pepper

1 pork tenderloin (about 1¼ pounds)

½ medium savoy cabbage, cored and cut into ¼-inch slices (about 6 cups)

1 small leek, cut in half lengthwise then cut crosswise into ¼-inch diagonal slices

1 to 2 teaspoons cider vinegar

1. Preheat oven to 450°F. Brush baking sheet with oil.

2. Combine salt, garlic powder, thyme and pepper in small bowl; mix well. Stir in ¼ cup oil until well blended. Brush pork with about 1 tablespoon oil mixture, turning to coat all sides.

3. Combine cabbage and leek in large bowl. Drizzle with remaining oil mixture; toss to coat. Spread on prepared baking sheet; top with pork.

4. Roast about 25 minutes or until pork is 145°F, stirring cabbage mixture halfway through cooking time. Remove pork to cutting board; tent with foil and let stand 10 minutes before slicing. Add vinegar to cabbage mixture; stir to blend.

TIP: If you can't find savoy cabbage, you can substitute regular green cabbage but it may take slightly longer to cook. If the cabbage is not crisp-tender when the pork is done, return the vegetables to the oven for 10 minutes or until crisp-tender.

SERVING SUGGESTION: Serve with roasted red potatoes.

BBQ CHICKEN SKILLET PIZZA

MAKES 4 TO 6 SERVINGS

---

1 **pound frozen bread dough, thawed**

1 **tablespoon olive oil**

2 **cups shredded cooked chicken***

¾ **cup barbecue sauce, divided**

¼ **cup (1 ounce) shredded mozzarella cheese**

¼ **cup thinly sliced red onion**

½ **cup (2 ounces) shredded smoked Gouda**

Chopped fresh cilantro (optional)

Use a rotisserie chicken for best flavor and convenience.

---

1. Preheat oven to 425°F. Roll out dough into 15-inch circle on lightly floured surface. Brush oil over bottom and side of large (12-inch) cast iron skillet; place in oven 5 minutes to preheat.

2. Combine chicken and ½ cup barbecue sauce in medium bowl; toss to coat. Remove hot skillet from oven; press dough into bottom and about 1 inch up side of skillet.

3. Spread remaining ¼ cup barbecue sauce over dough. Sprinkle with mozzarella cheese; top with chicken mixture. Sprinkle with half of onion and Gouda cheese; top with remaining onion.

4. Bake 25 minutes or until crust is golden brown. Garnish with cilantro.

TUNA TOMATO CASSEROLE

MAKES 6 SERVINGS

2 cans (6 ounces each) tuna, drained and flaked

1 cup mayonnaise

1 onion, finely chopped

¼ teaspoon salt

¼ teaspoon black pepper

1 package (12 ounces) wide egg noodles, cooked according to package directions

8 to 10 plum tomatoes, sliced ¼ inch thick

1 cup (4 ounces) shredded Cheddar or mozzarella cheese

1. Preheat oven to 375°F.

2. Combine tuna, mayonnaise, onion, salt and pepper in medium bowl; mix well. Place drained noodles in large bowl.

3. Gently stir tuna mixture into noodles until well blended. Layer half of noodle mixture, half of tomatoes and half of cheese in 13×9-inch baking dish; press down slightly. Repeat layers.

4. Bake 20 minutes or until cheese is melted and casserole is heated through.

SLOW COOKER MEALS

CHEESY BROCCOLI CASSEROLE

MAKES 4 TO 6 SERVINGS

---

2 packages (10 ounces each) frozen chopped broccoli, thawed

1 can (10¾ ounces) condensed cream of potato soup, undiluted

1¼ cups (5 ounces) shredded sharp Cheddar cheese, divided

¼ cup minced onion

1 teaspoon hot pepper sauce

1 cup crushed potato chips or saltine crackers

---

1. Lightly grease slow cooker. Combine broccoli, soup, 1 cup cheese, onion and hot pepper sauce in slow cooker; mix well.

2. Cover; cook on LOW 5 to 6 hours or on HIGH 2½ to 3 hours.

3. Sprinkle chips and remaining ¼ cup cheese over broccoli mixture. Cook, uncovered, on LOW 30 to 60 minutes or until cheese is melted.

LAYERED MEXICAN-STYLE CASSEROLE

MAKES 6 SERVINGS

2 cans (about 15 ounces each) hominy, drained*

1 can (about 15 ounces) black beans, rinsed and drained

1 can (about 14 ounces) diced tomatoes with garlic, basil and oregano

1 cup thick and chunky salsa

1 can (6 ounces) tomato paste

½ teaspoon ground cumin

3 (9-inch) flour tortillas

2 cups (8 ounces) shredded Monterey Jack cheese

¼ cup sliced black olives

*Hominy is corn that has been treated to remove the germ and hull. It can be found with the canned vegetables or beans in most supermarkets.

1. Prepare foil handles (see below). Spray slow cooker with nonstick cooking spray.

2. Combine hominy, beans, tomatoes, salsa, tomato paste and cumin in large bowl.

3. Press 1 tortilla in bottom of slow cooker. (Edges of tortilla may turn up slightly.) Top with one third of hominy mixture and one third of cheese. Repeat layers. Press remaining tortilla on top. Top with remaining hominy mixture. Set aside remaining cheese.

4. Cover; cook on LOW 6 to 8 hours. Sprinkle with remaining cheese and olives. Cover; let stand 5 minutes. Pull out tortilla stack with foil handles.

FOIL HANDLES: Tear off three (18×2-inch) strips of heavy-duty foil or use regular foil folded to double thickness. Crisscross foil strips in spoke design and place into slow cooker to make lifting of tortilla stack easier.

KOREAN BEEF SHORT RIBS

MAKES 6 SERVINGS

---

4 to 4½ pounds beef short ribs

¼ cup chopped green onions

¼ cup tamari or soy sauce

¼ cup beef broth or water

1 tablespoon packed brown sugar

2 teaspoons minced fresh ginger

2 teaspoons minced garlic

½ teaspoon black pepper

2 teaspoons dark sesame oil

Hot cooked rice or linguini pasta

2 teaspoons sesame seeds, toasted

---

1. Place ribs in 5-quart slow cooker. Combine green onions, tamari, broth, brown sugar, ginger, garlic and pepper in medium bowl; mix well and pour over ribs. Cover; cook on LOW 7 to 8 hours or until ribs are fork-tender.

2. Remove ribs from cooking liquid. Cool slightly. Trim excess fat. Cut rib meat into bite-size pieces, discarding bones and fat.

3. Let cooking liquid stand 5 minutes to allow fat to rise. Skim off fat.

4. Stir sesame oil into liquid. Return beef to slow cooker. Cover; cook 15 to 30 minutes or until hot.

5. Serve with rice; garnish with sesame seeds.

VARIATION: Three pounds boneless short ribs can be substituted for beef short ribs.

POLENTA-STYLE CORN CASSEROLE

MAKES 6 SERVINGS

---

1 can (about 14 ounces) vegetable broth

½ cup cornmeal

1 can (7 ounces) corn, drained

1 can (4 ounces) diced green chiles, drained

¼ cup diced red bell pepper

½ teaspoon salt

¼ teaspoon black pepper

1 cup (4 ounces) shredded Cheddar cheese

---

1. Pour broth into slow cooker. Whisk in cornmeal. Stir in corn, chiles, bell pepper, salt and black pepper. Cover; cook on LOW 4 to 5 hours or on HIGH 2 to 3 hours.

2. Stir in cheese. Cook, uncovered, on LOW 15 to 30 minutes or until cheese is melted.

SERVING SUGGESTION: Divide cooked corn mixture into lightly greased individual ramekins or spread in pie plate; cover and refrigerate. Serve at room temperature or warm in oven or microwave.

CHICKEN IN HONEY SAUCE

MAKES 4 TO 6 SERVINGS

---

4 to 6 boneless skinless chicken breasts
  Salt and black pepper
2 cups honey
1 cup soy sauce

½ cup ketchup
¼ cup oil
2 cloves garlic, minced
  Sesame seeds (optional)

---

1. Place chicken in slow cooker; season with salt and pepper.

2. Combine honey, soy sauce, ketchup, oil and garlic in medium bowl. Pour over chicken. Cover; cook on LOW 6 to 8 hours or on HIGH 3 to 4 hours.

3. Garnish with sesame seeds before serving.

ITALIAN-STYLE POT ROAST

MAKES 6 TO 8 SERVINGS

2 teaspoons minced garlic

1 teaspoon salt

1 teaspoon dried basil

1 teaspoon dried oregano

¼ teaspoon red pepper flakes

1 boneless beef bottom round or chuck roast (2½ to 3 pounds)

1 onion, quartered and thinly sliced

1½ cups tomato-basil or marinara pasta sauce

2 cans (about 15 ounces each) cannellini or Great Northern beans, rinsed and drained

¼ cup thinly sliced fresh basil or chopped Italian parsley

1. Combine garlic, salt, dried basil, oregano and red pepper flakes in small bowl; rub over roast.

2. Place half of onion slices in slow cooker. Cut roast in half crosswise. Place half of roast over onion slices; top with remaining onion slices and other half of roast. Pour pasta sauce over roast. Cover; cook on LOW 8 to 9 hours or until roast is fork-tender.

3. Remove roast to cutting board; tent with foil. Let liquid in slow cooker stand 5 minutes. Skim off fat.

4. Turn slow cooker to HIGH. Stir beans into liquid. Cover; cook 15 to 30 minutes or until beans are heated through. Carve roast across grain into thin slices. Serve with bean mixture and fresh basil.

QUINOA & VEGETABLE MEDLEY

MAKES 6 SERVINGS

2 medium sweet potatoes, cut into ½-inch-thick slices

1 medium eggplant, peeled and cut into ½-inch cubes

1 medium tomato, cut into wedges

1 large green bell pepper, sliced

1 small onion, cut into wedges

½ teaspoon salt

¼ teaspoon black pepper

¼ teaspoon ground red pepper

1 cup uncooked quinoa

2 cloves garlic, minced

½ teaspoon dried thyme

¼ teaspoon dried marjoram

2 cups water or fat-free reduced-sodium vegetable broth

1. Coat slow cooker with nonstick cooking spray. Combine sweet potatoes, eggplant, tomato, bell pepper, onion, salt, black pepper and red pepper in slow cooker; toss to coat.

2. Meanwhile, place quinoa in fine-mesh strainer; rinse well under cold running water. Add to vegetable mixture. Stir in garlic, thyme, marjoram and broth. Cover; cook on LOW 5 hours or on HIGH 2½ hours until quinoa is tender and broth is absorbed.

CLASSIC BEEF & NOODLES

MAKES 8 SERVINGS

2 pounds cubed beef stew meat,
    browned in 1 tablespoon vegetable
    oil and drained
¼ pound mushrooms, sliced into halves
2 tablespoons chopped onion
2 cloves garlic, minced
1 teaspoon salt
1 teaspoon dried oregano
½ teaspoon black pepper

¼ teaspoon dried marjoram
1 bay leaf
1½ cups beef broth
⅓ cup dry sherry
1 cup (8 ounces) sour cream
½ cup all-purpose flour
¼ cup water
4 cups hot cooked noodles

1. Combine beef, mushrooms, onion, garlic, salt, oregano, pepper, marjoram and bay leaf in slow cooker. Pour in broth and sherry. Cover; cook on LOW 8 to 10 hours or on HIGH 4 to 5 hours. Remove and discard bay leaf.

2. Combine sour cream, flour and water in small bowl. Stir about 1 cup liquid from slow cooker into sour cream mixture. Add mixture to slow cooker. Cook, uncovered, on HIGH 30 minutes or until thickened and bubbly. Serve over noodles. Garnish as desired.

ZESTY CHICKEN & RICE SUPPER

MAKES 2 TO 4 SERVINGS

- **2 boneless skinless chicken breasts, cut into 1-inch pieces**
- **2 large green bell peppers, chopped**
- **1 small onion, chopped**
- **1 can (about 28 ounces) diced tomatoes, undrained**
- **1 cup uncooked rice**

- **1 cup water**
- **1 package (about 1 ounce) taco seasoning mix**
- **1 teaspoon salt**
- **1 teaspoon black pepper**
- **1 teaspoon ground red pepper**
- **Shredded Cheddar cheese (optional)**

Combine all ingredients except cheese in slow cooker; mix well. Cover; cook on LOW 6 to 8 hours or on HIGH 3 to 4 hours. Garnish with cheese.

BEAN RAGOÛT WITH CILANTRO-CORNMEAL DUMPLINGS

MAKES 6 SERVINGS

2 cans (about 14 ounces each) diced tomatoes

1 can (about 15 ounces) pinto or kidney beans, rinsed and drained

1 can (about 15 ounces) black beans, rinsed and drained

1½ cups chopped red bell peppers

1 onion, chopped

2 zucchini, sliced

½ cup chopped green bell pepper

½ cup chopped celery

1 poblano pepper, seeded and chopped*

2 cloves garlic, minced

3 tablespoons chili powder

2 teaspoons ground cumin

1 teaspoon dried oregano

¼ teaspoon salt

⅛ teaspoon black pepper

Cilantro-Cornmeal Dumplings (recipe follows)

*Poblano peppers can sting and irritate the skin, so wear rubber gloves when handling peppers and do not touch your eyes.

1. Combine tomatoes, beans, red bell peppers, onion, zucchini, green bell pepper, celery, poblano pepper, garlic, chili powder, cumin, oregano, salt and black pepper in slow cooker; mix well. Cover; cook on LOW 7 to 8 hours.

2. Prepare dumplings 1 hour before serving. Turn slow cooker to HIGH. Drop dumplings by level tablespoonfuls (larger dumplings will not cook properly) on top of ragoût. Cover; cook 1 hour or until toothpick inserted into dumplings comes out clean.

CILANTRO-CORNMEAL DUMPLINGS

¼ cup all-purpose flour	1 tablespoon shortening
¼ cup yellow cornmeal	1 tablespoon shredded Cheddar cheese
½ teaspoon baking powder	2 teaspoons minced fresh cilantro
¼ teaspoon salt	¼ cup milk

Mix flour, cornmeal, baking powder and salt in medium bowl. Cut in shortening with pastry blender or two knives until mixture resembles coarse crumbs. Stir in cheese and cilantro. Pour milk into flour mixture; stir just until dry ingredients are moistened.

ON THE SIDE

ROASTED POTATOES AND PEARL ONIONS

MAKES 8 SERVINGS

---

3 pounds red potatoes, scrubbed and cut into 1½-inch pieces

1 package (10 ounces) pearl onions, peeled

2 tablespoons olive oil

2 teaspoons dried basil or thyme

1 teaspoon paprika

¾ teaspoon salt

¾ teaspoon dried rosemary

¾ teaspoon black pepper

---

1. Preheat oven to 400°F. Spray large shallow roasting pan* with nonstick cooking spray.

2. Combine potatoes and onions in prepared pan. Drizzle with oil; toss to coat. Combine basil, paprika, salt, rosemary and pepper in small bowl; mix well. Sprinkle over vegetables; toss to coat. Spread in single layer.

3. Roast 20 minutes. Stir vegetables; roast 15 to 20 minutes or until potatoes are browned and tender when pierced with fork.

Do not use glass baking dish or potatoes will not brown.

HERBED CAULIFLOWER CASSEROLE

MAKES 5 SERVINGS

---

5 cups cauliflower florets (about 1¼ pounds)

1 tablespoon margarine, melted

1 small red bell pepper, cut into quarters

2 tablespoons water

3 large tomatoes, peeled, seeded and coarsely chopped

2 to 3 teaspoons chopped fresh tarragon

½ teaspoon chopped fresh parsley

⅓ cup (9 to 10) coarsely crushed unsalted saltine crackers

---

1. Preheat oven to 450°F.

2. Toss cauliflower with margarine in shallow baking dish or large sheet pan; spread cauliflower and bell pepper, cut sides down, in single layer. Add water to baking dish.

3. Bake 15 minutes. *Reduce oven temperature to 425°F.*

4. Bake 25 to 28 minutes or until cauliflower is tender and golden brown and bell pepper skin is blistered. Remove bell pepper pieces to plate. *Reduce oven temperature to 400°F.*

5. Remove and discard skin from bell pepper. Place tomatoes and bell pepper in food processor; process until smooth. Add tarragon and parsley; process until blended. Pour tomato sauce over cauliflower.

6. Bake 10 minutes or until hot and bubbly. Sprinkle with cracker crumbs just before serving.

CHEESY GREEN BEAN CASSEROLE

MAKES 6 SERVINGS

¾ cup milk

2 teaspoons all-purpose flour

1 teaspoon dried minced onion

½ teaspoon black pepper

1 package (16 ounces) frozen cut green beans, thawed

1 cup (4 ounces) shredded Cheddar cheese, divided

¼ cup seasoned dry bread crumbs

---

1. Preheat oven to 350°F.

2. Whisk milk, flour, dried onion and pepper in medium bowl until well blended. Pour into 1½-quart baking dish. Stir in green beans and ½ cup cheese.

3. Bake, uncovered, 25 minutes. Sprinkle with remaining ½ cup cheese and bread crumbs. Bake 5 minutes or until cheese is melted.

SKILLET ROASTED ROOT VEGETABLES

MAKES 4 SERVINGS

1 sweet potato, peeled, cut in half lengthwise and cut crosswise into ½-inch slices

1 large red onion, cut into 1-inch wedges

2 parsnips, cut diagonally into 1-inch slices

2 carrots, cut diagonally into 1-inch slices

1 turnip, peeled, cut in half and then cut into ½-inch slices

2½ tablespoons olive oil

1½ tablespoons honey

1½ tablespoons balsamic vinegar

1 teaspoon coarse salt

1 teaspoon dried thyme

¼ teaspoon ground red pepper

¼ teaspoon black pepper

1. Preheat oven to 400°F.

2. Combine all ingredients in large bowl; toss to coat. Spread vegetables in single layer in large (12-inch) cast iron skillet. Roast 1 hour or until vegetables are tender, stirring once halfway through cooking time.

SWEET POTATO AND APPLE CASSEROLE

MAKES 9 SERVINGS

- **1 cup all-purpose flour**
- **¾ cup (1½ sticks) butter, melted, divided**
- **½ cup packed brown sugar**
- **½ teaspoon salt**
- **½ teaspoon ground cinnamon**
- **¼ teaspoon ground nutmeg**
- **¼ teaspoon ground cardamom**
- **2 pounds sweet potatoes, peeled, halved lengthwise and thinly sliced**
- **2 Granny Smith apples, peeled, cored, halved lengthwise and thinly sliced**

---

1. Preheat oven to 375°F. Spray 2-quart baking dish with nonstick cooking spray.

2. Combine flour, ½ cup butter, brown sugar, ½ teaspoon salt, cinnamon, nutmeg and cardamom in medium bowl until well blended.

3. Arrange sweet potatoes and apples in prepared baking dish. Drizzle with remaining ¼ cup butter; season lightly with additional salt.

4. Crumble topping over sweet potatoes and apples. Bake 35 to 40 minutes or until topping is brown and potatoes and apples are tender.

BROCCOLI CASSEROLE

MAKES 4 SERVINGS

---

1 package (about 6 ounces) stuffing mix

1 can (10¾ ounces) condensed cream of mushroom soup, undiluted

1 package (10 ounces) frozen chopped broccoli, thawed

½ small onion, chopped

½ cup (2 ounces) shredded mozzarella or Cheddar cheese

---

1. Preheat oven to 350°F. Grease 2-quart casserole dish.

2. Prepare stuffing mix according to package directions. Add soup, broccoli and onion; mix well. Pour into prepared dish. Sprinkle with cheese.

3. Bake 30 minutes or until heated through and cheese melts.

ROASTED VEGETABLE SALAD WITH CAPERS AND WALNUTS

MAKES 6 TO 8 SERVINGS

---

1 pound small Brussels sprouts, trimmed

1 pound unpeeled small Yukon Gold potatoes, halved

¼ teaspoon salt

¼ teaspoon black pepper

¼ teaspoon dried rosemary

5 tablespoons olive oil, divided

1 red bell pepper, cut into bite-size pieces

¼ cup walnuts, coarsely chopped

2 tablespoons capers, drained

1½ tablespoons white wine vinegar

---

1. Preheat oven to 400°F.

2. Slash bottoms of Brussels sprouts; place in shallow roasting pan. Add potatoes; sprinkle with salt, black pepper and rosemary. Drizzle with 3 tablespoons oil; toss to coat. Roast 20 minutes. Stir in bell pepper; roast 15 minutes or until tender. Remove to large bowl; stir in walnuts and capers.

3. Whisk remaining 2 tablespoons oil and vinegar in small bowl until blended. Pour over salad; toss to coat. Serve at room temperature.

MAKE AHEAD TIP: Prepare in advance; cover and refrigerate up to 1 day. Serve at room temperature.

GLAZED PARSNIPS AND CARROTS

MAKES 6 SERVINGS

---

1 pound parsnips (2 large or 3 medium)

1 package (8 ounces) baby carrots

1 tablespoon canola oil

   Salt and black pepper

¼ cup orange juice

1 tablespoon butter

1 tablespoon honey

⅛ teaspoon ground ginger

---

1. Preheat oven to 425°F. Peel parsnips; cut into wedges to match size of baby carrots.

2. Spread vegetables in shallow roasting pan. Drizzle with oil and season with salt and pepper; toss to coat. Bake 30 to 35 minutes or until fork-tender.

3. Combine orange juice, butter, honey and ginger in small bowl. Pour over vegetables; bake 1 to 2 minutes or until glazed.

TOMATO, POTATO AND BASIL SKILLET

MAKES 4 SERVINGS

---

1 tablespoon olive oil, divided

3 cups sliced potatoes

⅓ cup minced fresh basil

2 whole eggs

2 egg whites

2 tablespoons fat-free (skim) milk

1 tablespoon Dijon mustard

1 teaspoon dry mustard

½ teaspoon salt

¼ teaspoon black pepper

2 cups sliced plum tomatoes

---

1. Heat 1½ teaspoons oil in medium nonstick skillet over medium heat until hot. Layer half of potato slices in skillet. Cover and cook 3 minutes or until lightly browned. Turn potatoes and cook, covered, 3 minutes or until lightly browned. Remove potatoes from skillet. Repeat with remaining 1½ teaspoons oil and potatoes.

2. Arrange all potatoes in skillet. Sprinkle with basil. Whisk together eggs, egg whites, milk, mustards, salt and pepper in small bowl. Pour over potatoes. Arrange tomatoes over potato mixture. Reduce heat to low. Cover and cook 10 minutes or until eggs are set. Cut into four wedges to serve.

MEDITERRANEAN VEGETABLE BAKE

MAKES 4 TO 6 SERVINGS

---

1 small red onion

1 medium zucchini

1 small yellow squash

2 tomatoes, sliced

1 small eggplant, thinly sliced

1 large portobello mushroom, sliced

2 cloves garlic, finely chopped

3 tablespoons olive oil

2 teaspoons chopped fresh rosemary leaves

⅔ cup dry white wine

Salt and black pepper

---

1. Preheat oven to 350°F. Grease shallow casserole or 13×9-inch baking dish.

2. Spiral red onion, zucchini and yellow squash with thick spiral blade.* Arrange spiraled vegetables, tomatoes, eggplant and mushroom alternately in prepared casserole dish. Sprinkle evenly with garlic. Combine oil and rosemary in small bowl; drizzle over vegetables. Pour wine over vegetables; season with salt and pepper. Cover loosely with foil.

3. Bake 20 minutes. Uncover; bake 10 to 15 minutes or until vegetables are tender.

*If you don't have a spiralizer, slice vegetables into thin strips or small pieces.

SWEET ENDINGS

TURTLE DUMP CAKE

MAKES 12 TO 16 SERVINGS

---

1 **package (about 15 ounces) devil's food cake mix**

1 **package (4-serving size) chocolate instant pudding and pie filling mix**

1½ **cups milk**

1 **cup chopped caramels**

1 **cup semisweet chocolate chips**

½ **cup pecan pieces**

½ **teaspoon coarse salt (optional)**

---

1. Preheat oven to 350°F. Spray 13×9-inch baking pan with nonstick cooking spray.

2. Combine cake mix, pudding mix and milk in large bowl; beat 1 to 2 minutes or until well blended. Spread evenly in prepared pan; top with caramels, chocolate chips and pecans. Sprinkle with salt, if desired.

3. Bake 30 to 35 minutes or until toothpick inserted into center comes out clean. Cool in pan at least 15 minutes before serving.

PLUM-SIDE DOWN CAKES

MAKES 8 CAKES

---

2 tablespoons butter

3 tablespoons packed brown sugar

3 plums, sliced

½ cup granulated sugar

2 tablespoons shortening

1 egg

1 cup all-purpose flour

1 teaspoon baking powder

¼ teaspoon salt

⅓ cup low-fat (1%) milk

---

1. Preheat oven to 350°F. Spray eight standard (2½-inch) muffin cups with nonstick cooking spray.

2. Place butter in small microwavable bowl; microwave on LOW (30%) just until melted. Stir in brown sugar. Spoon evenly into prepared muffin cups. Arrange plum slices in bottom of each cup.

3. Beat granulated sugar and shortening in medium bowl with electric mixer at medium speed until fluffy. Beat in egg until well combined. Combine flour, baking powder and salt in small bowl; beat into shortening mixture. Add milk; beat until smooth. Spoon batter into prepared muffin cups, filling three fourths full. Place pan on baking sheet.

4. Bake 20 to 22 minutes or until toothpick inserted into centers comes out clean. Cool in pan 10 minutes. Run knife around each cup; invert onto wire rack to cool completely.

PECAN-RAISIN BREAD PUDDING

MAKES 6 SERVINGS

½ of a 1-pound loaf day-old French bread,* sliced ¾ inch thick

4 tablespoons (½ stick) butter, divided

¾ cup golden or dark raisins

¾ cup cholesterol-free egg substitute

1 cup thawed frozen unsweetened apple juice concentrate

2 cups low-fat (1%) milk

1 tablespoon vanilla

½ teaspoon ground cinnamon

¼ teaspoon ground nutmeg

¼ teaspoon salt

½ cup coarsely chopped pecans

No-sugar-added fruit spread, heated (optional)

Sour dough bread, Italian bread or one French bread baguette can be substituted.

1. Toast bread slices; spread with 2 tablespoons butter. Cut into ¾-inch pieces. Brush 1 tablespoon butter onto bottom and sides of shallow 1½-quart baking dish. Add bread and raisins; mix lightly. Combine egg substitute, apple juice concentrate, milk, vanilla, cinnamon, nutmeg and salt in medium bowl; mix until well blended. Pour over bread mixture; press down bread pieces to saturate. Let stand 20 minutes.

2. Preheat oven to 375°F. Place baking dish in larger shallow baking pan or roasting pan; add enough hot water to baking pan to come 1 inch up sides of dish. Bake 30 minutes. Melt remaining 1 tablespoon butter. Add pecans; toss lightly to coat. Sprinkle over pudding. Continue baking 8 to 10 minutes or until pecans are toasted and pudding is set. Cool on wire rack. Serve warm or at room temperature with fruit spread, heated 10 to 15 seconds, if desired.

DOUBLE BANANA DUMP CAKE

MAKES 9 SERVINGS

1 package (about 18 ounces) banana cake mix, plus ingredients to prepare mix

¾ cup chopped hazelnuts or sliced almonds, toasted*

1 banana, thinly sliced

4 tablespoons chocolate hazelnut spread, heated**

*To toast hazelnuts, spread in single layer on ungreased baking sheet. Bake in preheated 350°F oven 5 to 7 minutes or until light brown, stirring occasionally.

**Microwave on LOW (30%) about 1 minute or until pourable.

1. Preheat oven to 350°F. Spray 9-inch square baking pan with nonstick cooking spray.

2. Prepare cake mix according to package directions; stir in ½ cup hazelnuts. Spread half of batter in prepared pan. Top with banana slices; drizzle with 2 tablespoons chocolate hazelnut spread. Top with remaining half of batter; sprinkle with remaining ¼ cup hazelnuts and drizzle with remaining 2 tablespoons chocolate hazelnut spread.

3. Bake 25 to 30 minutes or until toothpick inserted into center comes out clean. Cool in pan 15 minutes before serving.

QUICK PEACH CRISP

MAKES 5 SERVINGS

---

4 **cups sliced peeled peaches or nectarines (about 4 large peaches or nectarines)**

3 **tablespoons cinnamon-sugar (see Tip)**

12 **to 14 pecan shortbread cookies,* coarsely chopped**

Or substitute 20 vanilla wafers.

---

1. Preheat oven to 350°F. Place peaches in 9-inch square baking dish. Add cinnamon-sugar; toss gently until well mixed. Sprinkle with cookies.

2. Bake 25 to 30 minutes or until peaches are tender and cookies are lightly browned.

TIP: Cinnamon-sugar is available in most large supermarkets. Look for it in the spice or baking section. However, you can easily make your own by mixing together 1 cup sugar and 1 tablespoon ground cinnamon. Store cinnamon-sugar in a glass jar. Sprinkle it on buttered toast or applesauce.

TROPICAL BREAD PUDDING WITH ORANGE SAUCE

MAKES 10 TO 12 SERVINGS

¾ **cup raisins**

3 **cups milk**

3 **eggs**

1 **cup sugar**

1 **cup shredded coconut**

⅔ **cup coarsely chopped walnuts**

3 **tablespoons butter, melted**

2 **tablespoons vanilla**

1 **teaspoon ground nutmeg**

1 **jar (8 ounces) maraschino cherries, undrained**

1 **can (11 ounces) mandarin orange segments, undrained**

1 **loaf (16 ounces) cinnamon-raisin bread**

Orange Sauce (recipe follows, optional)

---

1. Preheat oven to 350°F.

2. Lightly spray 13×9-inch baking pan with nonstick cooking spray.

3. Place raisins in small bowl. Pour boiling water over to cover. Let stand 2 to 3 minutes or until plump. Drain.

4. Combine raisins, milk, eggs, sugar, coconut, walnuts, butter, vanilla and nutmeg in large bowl; mix well. Add cherries and oranges with liquid; mix well.

5. Break bread into large pieces, about 2 inches square. Add bread pieces to milk mixture. Mixture should be moist but not soupy. Pour into prepared pan. Sprinkle with additional coconut, if desired.

6. Bake 1 hour to 1¼ hours or until knife inserted near center comes out clean. Serve with Orange Sauce, if desired.

ORANGE SAUCE

1½ cups powdered sugar

½ cup (1 stick) butter, melted

¼ cup whipping cream

1 egg yolk

2 tablespoons orange-flavored liqueur

1. Combine powdered sugar, butter and cream in medium saucepan. Add egg yolk; mix well with wire whisk. Cook over medium heat, stirring constantly, until thickened.

2. Remove from heat and add liqueur. Let cool slightly.

PEACH CRANBERRY UPSIDE-DOWN DUMP CAKE

MAKES 12 TO 16 SERVINGS

¼ cup (½ stick) butter, melted

½ cup packed brown sugar

3 cups thawed frozen or canned peach slices (thick slices cut in half)

2 cups fresh cranberries

1 package (about 15 ounces) yellow cake mix, plus ingredients to prepare mix

1. Preheat oven to 350°F. Spray two 9-inch round cake pans with nonstick cooking spray.

2. Divide butter and brown sugar between prepared pans; spread evenly over bottoms of pans. Arrange peach slices over butter mixture; sprinkle with cranberries.

3. Prepare cake mix according to package directions. Spread half of batter over fruit in each pan.

4. Bake 30 to 35 minutes or until toothpick inserted into centers comes out clean. Cool 5 minutes; invert onto serving plates. Cool at least 30 minutes before cutting.

ORANGE CRANBERRY DUMP CAKE

MAKES 12 SERVINGS

---

1 package (about 15 ounces) yellow cake mix

4 eggs

¾ cup orange juice

½ cup canola or vegetable oil

¼ cup water

1 cup dried cranberries

Powdered sugar (optional)

---

1. Preheat oven to 350°F. Grease and flour 12-cup (10-inch) bundt pan.

2. Combine cake mix, eggs, orange juice, oil and water in large bowl; beat 1 to 2 minutes or until well blended. Stir in cranberries. Pour batter into prepared pan.

3. Bake about 40 minutes or until toothpick inserted near center comes out clean. Cool in pan 10 minutes; invert onto wire rack to cool completely. Sprinkle with powdered sugar, if desired.

CARAMEL APPLE BREAD PUDDING WITH CINNAMON CREAM

MAKES 16 SERVINGS

1 package (12 ounces) frozen escalloped apples, thawed

8 eggs, lightly beaten

2 cups milk

2 cups half-and-half

1 cup sugar

½ cup (1 stick) butter, melted

2 teaspoons baking powder

1½ teaspoons ground cinnamon, divided

1 teaspoon vanilla

1 loaf (16 ounces) challah or any sweet bread, cut into ¾-inch cubes

2 cups vanilla ice cream

1 jar (about 12 ounces) caramel ice cream topping

1. Preheat oven to 350°F. Spray 13×9-inch baking pan with nonstick cooking spray.

2. Combine apples, eggs, milk, half-and-half, sugar, butter, baking powder, 1 teaspoon cinnamon and vanilla in large bowl; mix well. Gently fold in bread cubes. Pour into prepared pan.

3. Bake 50 minutes or until set. Cool in pan 20 minutes. Meanwhile, microwave ice cream in medium microwavable bowl on HIGH about 30 seconds or until partially melted. Stir until smooth. Stir in remaining ½ teaspoon cinnamon.

4. Drizzle warm bread pudding with caramel sauce; serve with cinnamon ice cream mixture.

BAKED PEARS

MAKES 4 SERVINGS

---

2 medium ripe Bosc pears, peeled,
   halved lengthwise and cored

1 tablespoon sugar

¼ teaspoon ground cinnamon

2 teaspoons butter

½ cup pear juice

3 gingersnap cookies, crushed

---

1. Preheat oven to 375°F. Place pear halves, cut sides up, in glass baking dish; do not crowd. Combine sugar and cinnamon in small bowl; sprinkle over pears. Place ½ teaspoon butter in each pear cavity. Pour juice into baking dish.

2. Bake pears 30 minutes, basting after 15 minutes. Sprinkle with crushed gingersnaps; bake 10 minutes.

INDEX

QUINOA & VEGETABLE MEDLEY
(page 142)

METRIC CONVERSION CHART

VOLUME MEASUREMENTS (dry)

1/8 teaspoon = 0.5 mL
1/4 teaspoon = 1 mL
1/2 teaspoon = 2 mL
3/4 teaspoon = 4 mL
1 teaspoon = 5 mL
1 tablespoon = 15 mL
2 tablespoons = 30 mL
1/4 cup = 60 mL
1/3 cup = 75 mL
1/2 cup = 125 mL
2/3 cup = 150 mL
3/4 cup = 175 mL
1 cup = 250 mL
2 cups = 1 pint = 500 mL
3 cups = 750 mL
4 cups = 1 quart = 1 L

VOLUME MEASUREMENTS (fluid)

1 fluid ounce (2 tablespoons) = 30 mL
4 fluid ounces (1/2 cup) = 125 mL
8 fluid ounces (1 cup) = 250 mL
12 fluid ounces (1 1/2 cups) = 375 mL
16 fluid ounces (2 cups) = 500 mL

WEIGHTS (mass)

1/2 ounce = 15 g
1 ounce = 30 g
3 ounces = 90 g
4 ounces = 120 g
8 ounces = 225 g
10 ounces = 285 g
12 ounces = 360 g
16 ounces = 1 pound = 450 g

DIMENSIONS

1/16 inch = 2 mm
1/8 inch = 3 mm
1/4 inch = 6 mm
1/2 inch = 1.5 cm
3/4 inch = 2 cm
1 inch = 2.5 cm

OVEN TEMPERATURES

250°F = 120°C
275°F = 140°C
300°F = 150°C
325°F = 160°C
350°F = 180°C
375°F = 190°C
400°F = 200°C
425°F = 220°C
450°F = 230°C

BAKING PAN SIZES

Utensil	Size in Inches/Quarts	Metric Volume	Size in Centimeters
Baking or	8×8×2	2 L	20×20×5
Cake Pan	9×9×2	2.5 L	23×23×5
(square or	12×8×2	3 L	30×20×5
rectangular)	13×9×2	3.5 L	33×23×5
Loaf Pan	8×4×3	1.5 L	20×10×7
	9×5×3	2 L	23×13×7
Round Layer	8×1½	1.2 L	20×4
Cake Pan	9×1½	1.5 L	23×4
Pie Plate	8×1¼	750 mL	20×3
	9×1¼	1 L	23×3
Baking Dish	1 quart	1 L	—
or Casserole	1½ quart	1.5 L	—
	2 quart	2 L	—